SOCIAL SCIENCES DIVISION
CHICAGO PUBLIC LIBRARY
400 SOUTH STATE STREET
CHICAGO, IL 60605

REF
HQ
1170
.G45
1996

HWLCSO

Chicago Public Library

D0142130

Chicago Public Library

C
P L

REFERENCE

Form 178 rev. 1-94

SOCIAL SCIENCES DIVISION
CHICAGO PUBLIC LIBRARY
400 SOUTH STATE STREET
CHICAGO, IL 60605

WOMEN'S HISTORY AND CULTURE
VOL. 9

WOMEN AND
FUNDAMENTALISM

GARLAND REFERENCE LIBRARY
OF THE HUMANITIES
VOL. 1516

Women's History and Culture

WOMEN AND FUNDAMENTALISM

Islam and Christianity

Shahin Gerami

GARLAND PUBLISHING, Inc.
New York & London / 1996

Copyright © 1996 by Shahin Gerami
All rights reserved

Library of Congress Cataloging-in-Publication Data

Gerami, Shahin.
    Women and fundamentalism : Islam and Christianity /
Shahin Gerami.
        p.   cm. — (Garland reference library of the
humanities ; vol. 1516) (Women's history and
culture ; vol. 9)
        Includes bibliographical references (p.   ) and index.
        ISBN 0-8153-0663-6 (alk. paper)
        1. Muslim women.   2. Women in fundamentalist
churches.   3. Women in Islam.   4. Islamic fundamentalism.
5. Religious fundamentalism.   I. Title.   II. Series.
III. Series: Women's history and culture ; 9.
HQ1170.G45   1996
305.48'6971—dc20   95-4925
                                                             CIP

Cover illustration: Identification picture of six-year-old girl on
entry into first grade taken in 1983 in Tehran, Iran, after the
Iranian Revolution

Printed on acid-free, 250-year-life paper
Manufactured in the United States of America

RO1293033955

REF
SOCIAL SCIENCES DIVISION
CHICAGO PUBLIC LIBRARY
400 SOUTH STATE STREET
CHICAGO, IL 60605

To the memory of my father,
and for
Manoucher and
Annahita

Contents

List of Figures and Tables

Figures

Tables

Prologue

This book grew out of a debate about the shifting position of Iranian women in the Islamic Republic of Iran. The fundamentalists in Iran managed to direct the flow of the revolutionary process toward an Islamic orientation. Since then, gender discourse has become an essential ingredient of the republic's legitimacy agenda. Meanwhile, in America the political conservatives and religious fundamentalists enjoyed the outcome of a fruitful marriage. One year after the Islamic Revolution of Iran, a conservative president, with the help of religious fundamentalists like Jerry Falwell of the Moral Majority, was elected to the White House. The interaction between American conservatism and Iranian fundamentalism haunted three American administrations, and the juxtaposition continues.

Currently, fundamentalist trends in many parts of the world, particularly in the Middle East, are shifting old alliances and challenging established assumptions. Fundamentalist movements from India to Algeria vie for attention. Modernized Egypt is struggling with one of the oldest fundamentalist movements in the region. There, fundamentalist groups are set to replace a secular Western-oriented government with an Islamic one. Women's rights and roles are central to all these cases. Women themselves are involved in the centrifugal forces, pro and con.

Gender issues, such as woman's role and place, her power in the family and the society are crucial components of both Islamic and Protestant fundamentalism. Women are active participants in the gender discourse within the fundamentalist context. In the United States, the Protestant fundamentalist movement has created a vocal conservative group of women who champion the merits of the patriarchal family, a moral society, and a conservative political agenda. In many Muslim Middle Eastern countries, women are organized around issues of female domesticity and a return to the Islamic tradition of family and morality.

While this book goes to press, Iran, Egypt, and the United States are experiencing their own version of political conservatism and religious legitimation. In all three, women and women's issues remain central to the state's legitimacy and political expediency.

In the aftermath of the Islamic revolution, a rich literature has grown up dealing specifically with the "question of women" and the republic's attention to repositioning urban middle class women. The literature on fundamentalism is rich with enthnographic and descriptive studies dealing with women's status in these movements. I was propelled by scientific curiosity and personal desire to gauge women's attitudes toward these trends. This study combines comparative qualitative and quantitative techniques to chart women's views of their social status as formulated within fundamentalist discourse in Iran, Egypt, and the United States.

Many have read, listened to, and helped me to shape the format of the book. Foremost among them is Valentine Moghadam, whom I am indebted to for her insightful comments and unfaltering support and friendship. An earlier version of chapter 4 appeared in *Identity Politics* (Westview Press, 1994) under her editorship. I have also benefited from critical evaluations by Victor Matthews and Mary Hegland. Martha Wilkerson and Doris Ewing gave unending support during a turbulent time in my life. David Hartmann helped with the survey of American women and listened, with a smile, always, to my occasional gripes about life and work. Bill Bultas, Jennifer Brymer, and Mohammad Arbabi assisted me with data analysis and typing of various drafts of the book.

Two small grants from Southwest Missouri State University and a sabbatical leave provided funds for traveling to Iran and time for writing. To my (ex) department head, Don

Landon, for supporting my various research adventures by writing supporting letters and accommodating class schedules, I owe sincere gratitude. In addition, I am grateful to the editors at Garland Publishing, who remained committed to the manuscript, despite some delays.

To Iranian, Egyptian, and American women who gave of their time and opened their hearts, I feel a sense of deep appreciation. Many Iranian women leaders braved the challenge of talking openly at a very sensitive time in 1989 and gave insights and information and provided names of their colleagues to contact. I am enormously indebted to women journalists and lawyers, who always found time in their busy schedules to update me on current women's issues in Iran. I would like to acknowledge the assistance of the staff and editorial board of *Zan-e-Rouz* magazine, who helped with publication of the Farsi language questionnaire in *Zan-e-Rouz* magazine.

My father, Hassan Gerami, remained an inspiration and a soul mate. Among other things, he helped with official contacts, data collection, and interpretation of complicated Islamic doctrinal issues. I wish he could have seen the final product. To the rest of my family in Iran, who provided me with an extensive network of women and officials, gave me shelter, good food, and engaging dinner table discussions, I say thank you and Salaam.

To Manoucher, for understanding my need to write, for providing time by taking care of Annahita, for your unspoken support, and for being there, always, I owe you more than Thank You.

Women and
Fundamentalism

CHAPTER ONE

Gender Role Paradigms

Division of labor, which is the essence of many social organizations, has invariably incorporated a sexually segregated pattern of social responsibilities and rights. Culturally defined sexual distinctions determine men's and women's political, economic, and spatial positions within the social organization. Religious ideologies that solidify these functions also promote gender identities that further reevaluate and redefine previously established sex roles. Current fundamentalist movements within Islam and Western Christianity promote reconstruction of rigid sex roles.

The rich literature of sex roles produces many models and analytical tools with which one can investigate an existing pattern. Any of them brings strengths and certain weak links. Invariably, these models rest upon some combination of a tripolar structure. One pole extrapolates a culture versus nature dichotomy in which culture supersedes nature and man subjugates woman. The second pole represents a sexual division of labor in which woman's labor in childbearing and rearing is subservient to man's labor in production and powermaking. The reproductive is subsumed by the productive. The third pole delineates a spatial dichotomy in which men control the public domain and women reign in the private sphere, with the public being the prominent one. These poles provide a hierarchical structure that brands women and their traits, labor, and products as inferior and secondary.

FIGURE 1.1

GENDER ROLE PARADIGMS

MALE

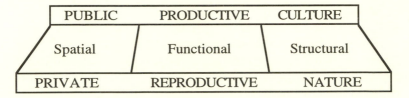

PUBLIC	PRODUCTIVE	CULTURE
Spatial	Functional	Structural
PRIVATE	REPRODUCTIVE	NATURE

FEMALE

Cultural Dichotomy

The foundation of the culture versus nature paradigm is a social structure in which the normative system is articulated by men and reinforced by both sexes. Men and women have distinct perceptions of their universe. Men define their universe in terms of boundaries of other groups and against natural vicissitudes. Women's world consists of their in-group and nature. Men's view stems from their interaction with other groups through cooperation and confrontation and their efforts to tame and exploit nature (Ardener, 1972). Women, on the other hand, have limited interaction with out-groups and thus are more introversive. Furthermore, their childbearing and rearing activities breed a view of nature that is inclusive. In sum, women's world includes the culture of the in-group and nature, while men's universe poses nature against culture. Men see nature as wild and as needing to be tamed and controlled. To them, women's reproductive power resembles the unravelling aspect of nature: wild and mysterious. Ardener suggests that for Bakweri men of Cameroon, "the problem of women" is that women work in what men consider the "wild": beyond the edge of the village, and their natural reproductive power is not controlled by men (1972:143–4). This association of women with nature and, thus, dark forces is well documented in the perception of women as witches in Europe and in their power of sorcery in many Eastern cultures (see Crapanzano, 1972). It is also reflected in the fear of menstrual blood and menstruating women by men of various cultures (see Ellman, 1968).

The association of men with culture is also revealed in the works of many Muslim theologians. The notion that man represents the norm, the regulated, and the systematic and that woman is representative of the destructive and untamed forces is reflected in the writings of Mottahari and al-Ghazzali. Islam views woman's sexuality as active in contrast to the Western perception of woman's sexuality as passive. This sexual creature is, thus, closer to nature (see Mernissi, 1987). In many Muslim Middle Eastern countries, a beautiful woman is called "Fitna," which means "chaos."

In the structural setting, man's burden toward women is analogous to the white man's burden toward the nonwhites. He is to capture, control, and then civilize them. Expecting less than satisfactory results, he must continually observe the "Other"— women and nonwhites.

Observers of the societies that are said to have a nature versus culture dichotomy of sex roles universally perceive culture to be the superior element (Ellman, 1968). Rogers (1978), however, criticizes such views as particularistic and not universally accepted. She suggests that these observers have generalized the Western middle-class preoccupation with women's childbearing to the other cultures (see also Ortner, 1974). In many peasant or tribal societies, women's childbearing is not a hindrance to their routine productive activities and child rearing is the responsibility of the older siblings or old members of the family. Furthermore, a view of women as wild and uncivilized contradicts their being perceived as moral and the keepers of the faith in many cultures.

Spatial Dichotomy

This constitutes a private domestic sphere that embraces women, their children, and their daily concerns. This may include only women and young children, or older men. Adults may engage in housekeeping and care giving or may participate in production of goods for the use of the family or in exchange for cash. Thus, the domestic may refer to a middle-class homemaker and her children in an industrialized community or an extended network of women, children, and older men in a collective household that includes their animals, their looms, and the family garden (see Aswad, 1967; Asad, 1970; Farrag, 1971).

The public/private domain distinction is reflected in the nomenclatures of many societies. For instance, the concepts of "home" and "work" are solidly ingrained in the cultural discourse of many Western societies. In other cultures, it may be "home" and "market" or "men's space" and "women's space" (Simmel, 1955). Therefore, any attempt to provide a universally applicable conceptualization of these constructs is futile and unnecessary.

There are those who, nevertheless, question the validity of these concepts and argue that they are products of the cultural bias of Western ethnographers. Two views predominate among the Western observers. One view is that the private is subservient to the public and that women's status is absolutely subservient to that of men. On the other side are those who maintain that this spatial distinction is a result of Western observers imposing their cultural constructs on the rest of the world (Rogers, 1978). According to Nelson (1974:560), "what becomes defined as the public and private spheres, however, are less the categorizations of the world by the actors living in these societies than they are the metaphors of the observers who are recording the actions of men and women in these societies."

Rogers claims that in peasant societies family is "the key political, economic and social unit" (Rogers, 1978:148). She further suggests that associating the private sphere with subjugation is purely speculative, while Rosaldo attributes women's subjugation to their being focused on child care and domestic activities (1974). On the other hand, mere engagement in the public sphere does not guarantee improved status, as the case of slaves indicates. Another example is feminine occupations in industrialized societies, which are conferred lower status than masculine occupations of the same type.

In formulating and distinguishing these spheres, power is often emphasized as the delineating factor (Lienhardt, 1972; Nelson, 1974). Douglas (1970:84) reports that women's "social relations certainly carry less weighty pressure than those which are also institutional in range. This is a social condition they share with serfs and slaves. Their place in the public structure of roles is clearly defined in relation to one or two points of reference, say in relation to husband and fathers" (see also Nelson, 1974). Similarly, Simpson-Hebert (1990), in her article on hospitality among Iranians, overlooks women's indirect power in the preparation and administration of family feasts, which she assumes serve only men's public and familial interests. In most studies, the public is associated with institutionalized power, that is, authority, and the private with mediated power, meaning influence and manipulation (Rosaldo, 1974; O'Brien, 1977; Rogers, 1978).

In modern times, the public authority has leaked into the domestic domain. The all-encompassing national governments regulate domestic affairs too, though to a lesser degree. Mandatory education of children, family planning, and minimum age of marriage are a few examples of state authority in the family that supersede man's power. As part of these regulations, states have granted women a few areas of authority or have codified their previous vestiges of power. For instance, eliminating or regulating polygamy, allowing women to seek divorce, providing free contraceptives and abortion, etc. are examples of women's authority over men's conduct in the private sphere.

By granting women authority in some areas, states have reduced women's need for manipulation. Similarly, states have codified men's power as well. Nevertheless, it is reductionist to base spatial distinction only on power. This paradigm is a multidimensional, dynamic, and dialectical structure that constitutes a division of labor, a normative order, and above all, a value structure. This value system requires male and female personality traits that embody the spatial dimension. It also promotes an ideal separation that must be observed through a complicated web of social norms.

The normative system regulates the minute nuances of the sexes' behavior, both in the public sphere and in the private sphere (Najmabadi, 1991). For instance, the notion of female modesty in these societies is an extension of the private domain. Even in the public domain, women's behavior is a reminder of their "natural" domain. In many large cities of the Middle East, women, veiled or unveiled (especially the latter), are bound by a code of modesty to remind them and others where their "true" habitat lies. Women are often harassed in the public sphere. While this may be due to sexual frustration of men, it makes women unwanted and uncomfortable in the public sphere. On the other hand, men who involve themselves in women's affairs are ridiculed by both sexes.

The division of labor is reflective of the functional paradigm. This system regards childbearing and rearing as women's natural primary function. Consequently, their role in the formal labor market, particularly in urban areas, is restricted. Indeed, where the formal labor force is predominantly in the public sphere, women's productive activity is severely mitigated by the spatial paradigm. Therefore, for the purpose of this research, the public sphere is defined in terms of the predominance of authority—including political, judicial, and coercive—and the formal labor market. Finally, the fluidity of the boundaries must be emphasized. The extent of segregation varies by culture, social class, urban or rural settings, and ethnic identity of the communities. For instance, the Armainian communities in the Middle East observe a spatial dichotomy that is markedly different from those of the Muslim and the Jewish communities.

Generally, spatial boundaries are somewhat exclusionary but not exclusive. Age by itself can be a delineating factor. Old or widowed women have more access to the public than younger or married child-bearing women. Men enter the domestic sphere at various points and are never entirely excluded. Many return to it permanently at old age, more so in modern times than before. Retired men, whether from agriculture or office work, stay at home and become part of the domestic sphere. A Saudi woman from Jeddah told the author "they [men] had their coffee shops and gatherings before, now many [of their friends] are dead or are abroad with their children and the coffee shops are closing because the younger generation do not go there, so they stay home with us causing grief."

Functional Paradigm

This is defined mostly in terms of women's reproductive capacity and its associated functions in the society. Margaret Mead (1963) and Murdock (1937, 1949) are the pioneers in conceptualizing sex-role specialization. Murdock provides the rich battery of sex-role specialization in foraging societies. He discerns patterns of "female compatible" and "male compatible" tasks based on physiological differences of the sexes. He contends that "physiological burdens of pregnancy and nursing handicap women" (1949:7). Men, free from such restrictions, can engage in activities requiring greater mobility and agility. This is reiterated by functionalists, who view sex roles as an efficient adaptation of the sex's physiology to the social environment. As Parsons and Bales state:

> In our opinion the fundamental explanation for allocation of the roles between the biological sexes lies in the fact that the bearing and early nursing of children establishes a strong and presumptive primacy of the relation of mother to the small child and this in turn establishes a presumption that the man who is exempted from these biological functions should specialize in the alternative direction. (Parsons and Bales, 1955:23)

Lévi-Strauss (1956) and his students suggest that when men and women specialize in different tasks in the society, it provides for reciprocity of the services between them. Such a mutual dependence generates a solid foundation for strong families. In the long run, the offspring of these families have higher fertility and survival rates.

The central factor in the functional paradigm is women's childbearing and rearing. In cases where women participate in hunting, like Mabuti pygmies of the African Congo, or the !Kung Bushmen where men and women both hunt and gather, an exception is made. It is suggested that in these societies, opportunities for hunting are nearby so this activity does not interfere with women's childbearing and rearing (Friedl, 1975). Another explanation may be that the society values hunting more than children. To assume that the children are an important force to organize the family and society around their survival has a modern Western ring to it. Furthermore, it assumes that parenting and especially mothering (not pregnancy) are natural rather than cultural behaviors. High rates of infanticide in foraging and agrarian societies, at least, cast a shadow on natural parental affection.

This perspective views the functional differentiation of the sexes as a natural truism. The concepts of "man the hunter" and "woman the gatherer" have been adapted to the modern time as "man the provider" and "woman the nurturer." Such an assumption requires an either/or sex-role identification. Indeed, feminine is the opposite of masculine, and one cannot be both (Murray, 1972; Slocum, 1975). In this system, men's and women's identities are delineated based on biological makeup. Women's identity is defined in terms of their perceived biological and psychological nature, which accordingly assigns their appropriate functions. The result is a hierarchical dichotomy delineating the feminine and masculine functions of the sexes. This sex-role ascription is part of a worldview with moral justification of social responsibilities and rights and an associated distributive system of rewards. In this system, man as the head of the household is the guardian of the established sex roles.

Comparative Analysis

The three poles of the functional, structural, and spatial are interrelated and interchangeable. At times, one is singled out as the basis of the other two dichotomies. Epstein maintains that "the association of women with nature and therefore, by anatomical analogy, with child care has long provided an excuse for excluding them from the political realm" (1988:14). Rosaldo suggests that "the opposition between domestic and public orientations (an opposition that must, in part, derive from nurturant capacities of women) provides the necessary framework for an examination of male and female roles in any society" (1974:24).

Indeed, the debate about functional and spatial dichotomies of sex-role allocation is extensive and, at times, contentious. It is analogous to the chicken-and-the-egg example. Were women assigned to the private domain and then their nurturing functions used to justify their restrictions, or was it their nurturing functions that made them sequestered in the private domain and thus secondary in terms of power and resources?

This tripolar structure is often reduced to spatial and functional dichotomies, subsuming the nature/culture dimension. Discussions of these dimensions have been conducted primarily by Western anthropologists, and the data have been overwhelmingly ethnographic. As far as the Muslim societies are concerned, the debate becomes even more complicated due to the unavailability of the female domain to many earlier ethnographers. Native Middle Eastern observers themselves disagree as to the significance of spatial segregation. For Mernissi, "Muslim sexuality is territorial: its regulatory mechanism consists primarily in strict allocation of space to each sex and an elaborate ritual for resolving the contradictions arising from the inevitable intersections of spaces" (1987:137; see also Sabbah, 1984). On the other hand, Altorki contends the private/public dichotomy is misleading and not supported by empirical research (1986:27).

The universal application of these dichotomies is problematic. The private/public debate is more appropriate and in tune with the Islamic culture and the functional debate more relevant to the Western Christian asymmetry.

Spatial/Functional Duality

The debate about women's role and place in Western Christianity dates back to the interpretation of Genesis, St. Paul's and St. Augustine's statements (Bullough, 1973; Elshtain, 1981). The issue is not gender roles. Man's role and place are not disputed, rather it is woman's existence, utility, and place that are questioned. Man's social existence is defined in relation to God, and woman's to man. Sex roles description compares woman's nature and potentials to those of man's to further illustrate woman's secondary status.

The story begins with Genesis, in which woman's destructive power is first exposed. For this she is condemned to the pain of childbirth and servitude to her husband:

> To the woman he said: I will greatly multiply your pain in childbirth, in pain you shall bring forth children, yet your desire shall be for your husband and he shall rule over you. (Genesis 1–5 in Mahowald, 1983:289–292)

In the same passage, the man is rebuked for "listening to the voice of" his wife and condemned to toil on a ground that is cursed because of him, all the days of his life (ibid.). Historically, the diffusion of Roman-Greek as well as Persian philosophies have influenced Western Christianity's definition of women as subservient and subversive.

Subordinate Social Existence

> But I want you to understand that the head of every man is Christ, the head of a woman is her husband. For a man ought not to cover his head, since he is the image and glory of God, but woman is the glory of man. For man was not made from woman, but woman from man. Neither was man created for woman but woman for man. (1 Corinthians 11 in Mahowald, 1983:300)

This idea has become ingrained in Western Christianity. While in recent years it has been reinterpreted by the New Christian Right to imply women's complimentary virtues (Schlafly, 1981), sexual inequality remains the essence of Western Christianity's approach to women's status (Falwell, 1980). This inferiority extends from family to society, denying women equal access to valued resources.

Sexual Subversiveness

Woman as daughter of Eve is a hindrance to man's true realization of his spirituality. She breeds and generates desires of the
flesh. To free their spirits, men need to denounce bodily plea-
sures. Sex is at the top of this list. However, having women
around makes men's asceticism difficult. Early Christians
blamed women for their sexual desires, and some even debated
woman's usefulness. Paul, in particular, comes close to suggesting that women are necessary evils; they are necessary for procreation but harmful to the Christians' salvation (1 Corinthians 7
in Mahowald, 1983:298–99).

The battle between spirit and flesh was generally lost in
favor of the flesh, and women were denounced as the culprits.
The faithful were instructed to engage in intercourse for
procreation and not pleasure. This misogynism permeates
Western Christianity. Bullough (1973:104) suggests that
asceticism "must have struck a responsive cord in Western
intellectual thought, or else there would not have been such a
widespread agreement."

Here, Christianity departs from the Islamic approach to
sex. While Islam regards and even encourages sex both for
reproduction and pleasure, Western Christianity views sex as an
undesirable but necessary human behavior. Both doctrines try to
regulate the sexual conduct of their followers. In this regulatory
capacity, they restrict and subjugate women. They regard men's
sexual drive as natural but admonish women for arousing as
well as satisfying their desires.

In Islamic societies, the cultural interpretation of women's
biological distinctions is cast in terms of the place of women in
society. By starting from woman's "natural" abilities, the Islamic
doctrine sequesters her in the private sphere, which in turn
restricts her functions. The result is a multidimensional
exclusionary practice that by all accounts is currently more
restrictive than in other patriarchies (White 1978; Marshall and
Stokes 1981). In Islamic societies, women's identity reflects
varied adaptations of these principles:

Biological determinism of woman's place

Woman's reproductive power has been used to justify her confinement to the private domain. Islamic jurists—sometimes influenced by Greek philosophers—have claimed that women are physically weaker, emotionally unstable, and intellectually inferior to men. Thus, they belong at home engaged in homemaking and child rearing (Gerami, 1989).

Woman's sexual power

Islamic texts abound with the declaration that woman's sexual power, left unchecked, is destructive to the Islamic social order. Man, with his primordial lust for woman, is no match for her alluring schemes. To safeguard the sanctity of the family and *ummat* (community), men must be saved from their insatiable search for sexual gratification (Sabbah, 1984). To this end, Islamic patriarchy confines women to the private domain and restricts their movement in public. Should women appear in public, they are required to observe dress and behavioral standards (*hijab*) that obscure their sexual identity. The extent of seclusion and the forms of *hijab* are subject to the culture, history, economy, and climate of a society or even a group.

Geographical segregation

Numerous examples in the language and folklore of Muslim societies confirm the idea of sex segregation (Hossain, 1988).[1] In Iran, in the traditional family, women are referred to as *manzel* (home), *andaruni* (inner section), etc. Many middle- and upper-class homes used to contain a *beruni* (outer house) where men resided, entertained, and conducted business, and an *andaruni*, which was the women's section.

Woman's function?

As a raison d'être and as a result of this segregated policy, woman's functions are limited to motherhood and housekeeping. While this may sound tautological, considering the philosophical exchange between Roman-Greek and Islamic patriarchies (Hassan, 1987), this is both the cause and effect of the seclusion.

According to *Shariat* (Islamic canon law) jurists, Allah created men and women differently and assigned each distinct responsibilities to be performed in their proper domain (Mottahari, 1974). Therefore, spatial separation that identifies each sex's functions leads to duplication of some functions. In orthodox Islamic doctrine, a woman has no legitimate function in the public domain, so feminine occupations of the Western system, such as secretarial work, nursing, and teaching boys, were performed by men and, despite postwar modernization, have remained intact to a large extent.

The doctrines of Islam and Western Christianity generally follow similar paths for controlling women's behavior (Doumato, 1991). It is only in the practical implementation of the restrictions that these doctrines part. While Islam prescribes spatial seclusion of women, Western Christianity recommends functional restriction. It is suggested that Jesus' teachings regarding women have been more progressive than the prevailing Judaic practices of the time (Bainton, 1957). The presence of women functionaries in the church organization also supports this claim. The same, however, can be deduced from early Islamic history.

What does, then, account for some discernable differences between the two traditions in terms of women's status? Two factors stand out. One is the specific ministerial functions designated for women in the early church organization that were later adopted by Western Christianity. Evangelism and charity were praised as women's virtues and allowed them limited presence in the public sphere (Bainton, 1957; Bullough, 1973:100). The second factor is promotion of virginity to control women's sexuality.[2]

Female virginity is valued in both traditions. Women's chastity is a major technique of social control in a patriarchy. It safeguards a man's bloodline and consequently his heirs. However, Christian virgins are conceptualized as asexual (Bullough, 1973:104). In Islam, virgins become asexual by being veiled. Unlike Islam, Christianity prescribes sex only for reproduction and does not attribute strong sexual power to women and insatiable sexual drive to men. Therefore, the urgency to seclude woman to make her asexual does not permeate Christian dogma. Rather, this system focuses on delineating woman's role within the family and safeguarding man's authority against intrusion by the other sex (Henning, 1974).

Indeed, these traditions have chosen slightly different paths to safeguard patriarchy: Western Christianity has denigrated sexuality and thus constructed virginity as asexual; Middle Eastern Islam has conceptualized female sexuality as destructive and thus constituted seclusion.

Compared to the Islamic seclusion, Christian virginity is less restrictive. Virgins can be at the service of the faith by evangelism, caring for, and healing of the faithful. Thus, a combination of three factors—denouncing sex for pleasure, asexual virgins, and women in evangelism—grants Christian women some legitimate functions in the public domain and thus more social mobility. This background can shed some light on the nurturing public functions of women in Western Christianity. In the home, women are at the service of men and children; in the community, they are at the service of the church. Neither in the home nor in the community do women claim an equal status with men.

Like the functional order, the Islamic spatial system is part of a social system of roles, responsibilities, and distributive rewards. It, too, limits and rejects women's equal right to political and economic resources. Furthermore, since the formal job sector is all in the public domain, particularly in cities, spatial segregation restricts women's economic opportunities more than the functional order. Youseff (1974) proposes that seclusion of Muslim women has affected their participation in the nonagricultural sector. Gerami (1988), in a cross-cultural study, shows that, after controlling for the effects of economic growth and modernization, Muslim women have lower labor force participation and higher fertility than Catholic women in Latin American countries.

It must be pointed out that plausible arguments can be made in favor of other typologies. The above dichotomies are not mutually exclusive. Some students of sex roles have applied the spatial distinction to the study of women's roles in America (Hargrove et al., 1985), while others have expanded it to include the Christian world in general. Thus, these categories serve as typology, not concrete boundaries. Indeed, the overlaps between the categories generate elastic boundaries that fluctuate with the cultural, economic, and sociopolitical conditions of societies. For instance, in Saudi Arabia a bank run by women ensures seclusion of women clientele, while Kuwaiti women enjoy greater freedom in the public environment (Bahry, 1982; Ramazani, 1985). In a cross-cultural study, Kagitcibasi (1986:487) found that "the similarities between Turkish and Greek family cultures and sex roles were much greater than those between Turkish and Indonesian family cultures and roles."

While postwar modernization relaxed sexual segregation in some Muslim countries, the rise of Islamic fundamentalism has resurrected spatial separation as the core of its ideal society. Similarly, in the United States, a strong fundamentalist movement since the late 1970s has refocused attention on women's roles in the society and the conflict between her familial obligations and her social aspirations. Indeed, these movements have raised questions about the proper role and place of women, and there is a strong support for these movements among women of each region.

In the West, the fundamentalist movement has created a vocal conservative group of women who champion the merits of the patriarchal family, a moral society, and a conservative political agenda. Describing the ideology of the new conservative movement in America, Klatch (1988:676) writes, "While male and female roles are each respected as essential and complementary components of God's plan, men are the spiritual leaders and decision makers in the family. It is women's role to support men in their position of higher authority through altruism and self-sacrifice." The family and not the individual is the basic social unit, with man in the position of authority and woman as the supportive agent of his decisions (Conover and Gray, 1983). As expressed by Jerry Falwell, "good husbands who are godly men are good leaders. Their wives and children want to follow them and be under their protection. The husband is to be the decision maker" (quoted in Klatch, 1987:44).

Similarly, in Islam, man's identity is defined by his social roles and woman's by her familial roles. In Muslim societies of the Middle East, Islamic fundamentalism has raised questions about the corruption of traditional culture, economic and cultural dependence on the West, assault on Islamic values, and usurpation of the extended family.

So far the bulk of evidence for the existence of a spatial separation of sexes has come from participant observation studies. The rising tide of religious fundamentalism in the United States, Iran, and Egypt provides a unique opportunity for a cross-cultural study of the spatial and functional paradigms. An empirical investigation of women's perception of their societal roles can shed light on the relevance of these paradigms when studying sex roles cross-culturally. Indeed, it is imperative to provide a definition of spatial versus functional distinctions by women themselves. Such research can also lay the foundation for a synthesis of the dichotomies based on any overlap that might be observed.

Basic Research Design

This is a comparative analysis of women's perception of their role and place within the context of religious fundamentalism in the United States, Egypt, and Iran. The few comparative studies of religious fundamentalism have not addressed women's role, which is often central to these movements.

Students of sex roles in Muslim countries have focused their attention on women's behavior, organizations, and participation in current Islamic movements (Bauer, 1983; Betteridge, 1983; Hegland, 1983). During the past decade, Middle Eastern women with Western educations have produced a fresh look into the lives, roles, and aspirations of their sisters (Altorki, 1986; Abu-Laughod, 1986). A survey of analyses of women's attitudes toward the changes in their proper role and place, as the call for a return to the "true" Islamic principles continues, will add a new dimension.

With respect to Protestant fundamentalism, works by Klatch (1987) and Conover and Gray (1983) have yielded firsthand knowledge of women's views of their role and place vis-à-vis Protestant fundamentalism. This research combines ethnographic and survey techniques to provide a cross-cultural understanding of religious fundamentalism and women's societal status.

The basic elements of the research design calls for four major questions to be addressed:

Women's Role versus Their Place

Western Christianity promotes a dual functional system in which women's primary function is procreation and homemaking. The new wave of Protestant fundamentalism in America reaffirms traditional family roles. Defeat of the Equal Rights Amendment, the antiabortion campaign, and the debate about homosexuals in the military reflect a campaign against any tampering with perceived ordained gender identities.

In the case of Islamic fundamentalism, serious attempts are being made to revive the spatial dichotomy of the private and public domains. Reinstitution of *Shariat* in many countries, veiling, and removal or harassment of women in the public domain are signs of a reinvigorated spatial allocation.

The first two questions then, address women's perception of their role and their place in the society within the context of religious fundamentalism:
1. Do women perceive a functional duality of the sex roles? (The extent of overlap between these roles)
2. Do women see a spatial segregation of the sexes? (The extent of their support for sex segregation)

Women's Relation to Power

The new fundamentalist movements reject the passivity of the old religious establishments and promote political activism of religious groups and organizations. Despite their call for a return to original scripture, religious fundamentalists do not seek replication of the early years of a religion; rather, they reformulate their religious ideology to further a political agenda. Leaders of these movements utilize the latest available technology and bureaucratic organization to spread their message, recruit new members, and establish a system legitimized by God. Whether the Moral Majority or Hezab-Allah, the participants see their mission as changing the mundane to match the ordained.

Women constitute a major section of the fundamentalists' cadres. Whether blocking an abortion clinic in America or enforcing the mandatory veil in Iran, women have joined the movement. There are also those who are mobilized against its spread and its mandate for women. The fundamentalist groups have brought women's issues to the forefront of the public debate, and, regardless of their support or opposition to the movement, women have become politicized and sensitized to women's issues as a political agenda. Even those who are passive bystanders have heard the debate and have been told to take charge of women and family issues. They have been told and have told others about the decline of morality, the rejection of the "true" faith, the threat to the family, the spread of decadence, and the evil plot to destroy the ordained fabric of their respective societies. Has this rhetoric and attention to women's issues imbued them with a greater sense of empowerment?

　　　3. How do women see their relation to power?

　　　(The extent of women's power in the family and society)

Feminism and Equality

Both movements have responded to feminism in a negative way. The Protestant fundamentalists are against what they see as the usurpation of the traditional family, erosion of moral values and removal of legal protection for women (Marshall, 1991). Islamic fundamentalism, in large part, is a response to Western incursion into the private domain. Postwar modernization expanded the labor market, reduced the power of *Shariat*, and relaxed spatial separation. Both movements are dedicated to stopping the feminist incursion and reaffirming women's "proper" status. Despite the leaders' attempts to return women to their proper role and place, the women participants have revised a new traditional status that is active and involved. We will address the issue of secular versus fundamentalist activism among women.

It is imperative to measure women's support for sexual equality and their group solidarity given the increased fundamentalists' rhetoric:

    4. What are women's responses to feminism?
    (The extent of their support for sexual equality)

This is a broad outline of the research questions addressed in the following chapters. Each chapter contains a section on method of data collection, the sample, and the analytical design. Next, we proceed to devise a gendered vision of religious fundamentalism.

NOTES

1. Hossain (1988) refers to "mardana" (men's section) and "Zanana" (women's section) in Bengali culture. These words are Farsi and used in the same manner in Iran, too.

2. An additional variable might be the integration of house and church in early Christianity. Up to the eighth or ninth generations, Christians worshiped in their homes, which allowed women immediate access to the sacred space. Muslims, on the other hand, were able to build mosques much earlier, which reduced women's access to the sacred space.

I am indebted to Professor Victor Matthews for pointing out this historical fact (for a detailed discussion see Campo, 1991).

CHAPTER TWO

A Gendered Vision of Religious Fundamentalism

Introduction

The surge of religious fundamentalism since the 1970s in culturally distinct areas of the globe has raised concern and interest among scholars and citizens. Regions of the world that have witnessed the rise of religious fundamentalism are as diverse as Algeria, Israel, the United States, Iran, and India. Indeed, the list goes far beyond these examples. Fundamentalism has been observed among the three major monolithic and many polytheistic religions of the world in countries in different stages of socioeconomic growth and diverse forms of political organizations. Both democracies and dictatorships have been affected by this phenomenon.

What is religious fundamentalism and under what sociohistorical conditions does it emerge? The following is a brief historical account of fundamentalism. Later, we will postulate a conceptual framework.

Historical Antecedent

The origin of fundamentalism goes back to American Protestantism as practiced on the frontier in the late 1800s. The structural changes occurring in America unsettled many inhabitants of the frontier. Industrialization and urban growth brought new inhabitants with different life styles and unfamiliar cultures. The new Irish immigrants introduced a culture and religion that was unfamiliar and threatening. Urban growth meant a pluralistic society with divergent groups closely mixing in institutions such as schools and the workplace. Labor unrest challenged the ideology of a fair and free society in the new land. Many (Chalafant et al., 1987; Riesebordt, 1993) have observed that fundamentalism was a frontier response to the encroaching city, with its alien sociocultural system that was viewed as heathen and threatening.

Also associated with urbanization was the economic transformation of American economy from agriculture to industry. The industrial growth fostered new ideas and a plurality of alternative beliefs. This had two consequences: the predominance of science and the spread of revisionism among biblical theologians. Biblical revisionists brought scientific techniques of evidence and verification to the Bible. On their examination table, the Bible became an historical document compiled through centuries, reflecting the cultural and historical markings of each revision, compilation, or translation. What was left was suitable for the urban intelligentsia. It was existentialist rather than spiritual (Bruce, 1992). It was disputable and disputed. The frontier Protestants had assumed the infallibility of the Bible. The cost of challenging the Bible in the face of other changes was serious.

"By 1910, the clash concerning nonliterary biblical interpretations, the Social Gospel ideology, and liberal theology had erupted into open controversy" (Chalafant et al., 1987:174). In an effort to stem the tide of revisionism, two wealthy California brothers, the Stewarts, arranged for the production and wide distribution of twelve pamphlets named *The Fundamentals*. These pamphlets, instead of diminishing the debate, widened its scope.

The impetus for the emergence of fundamentalism is attributed to the spread of modernism. "Fundamentalism came about as a self-conscious rejection of modernism in theology that sought to take into account the results of Biblical criticism, scientific discovery, and the general condition of the modern culture" (Webber, 1987:96). The credence given to science as the only valid and acceptable source of information posed a serious threat to traditional knowledge. Nowhere was this displayed better than in the Scopes trial of 1925 when William Jennings Bryan went on a collision course with modernism, as defended and presented by Clarence Darrow. By itself it was a minor affair, in which John Scopes, a biology teacher in Dayton, Tennessee, was said to have taught the evolution of species according to Darwin. Scopes himself could not recall whether he had done so. His prosecution propelled the discord between science and nonscience, in this case religion, into the public scene. Bryan could not defend the integrity of religion against the fact-oriented presentation of science.

This public humiliation had two consequences for the evangelicals: It reaffirmed their belief in the inerrancy of the Bible and led to their withdrawal from the public scene. They withdrew into their churches and their closed communities. Speer suggests that "on the way to becoming a 'beleaguered sect,' the legitimations for political activity gave way to an almost exclusive emphasis on regeneration" (1984:30). This retreat lasted until World War II. National events, such as the diffusion of public schools infused with rationalism and the scientific investigation of nature and the international spread of socialism, provided impetus for another reawakening.

There is a debate about the exact coinage of the word "fundamentalism" (see Sandeen, 1970; Marsden, 1980; Caplan, 1987). Mostly it is attributed to an editor of a Baptist paper who called upon the faithful to defend the "fundamentals of Protestantism" (Sandeen, 1970:246). These fundamentals are (a) biblical inerrancy; (b) the virgin birth of Jesus; (c) His substitutionary atonement; (d) His bodily resurrection; and (e) the authenticity of miracles. This list varies depending on historical and denominational proclamation (Sandeen, 1970).

Conceptual Framework

For our purposes here, I will adopt fundamentalism and dust off some of its popular appendages, beginning with a broad and general definition as the background for this research. I will first delineate the differences between fundamentalism and similar social phenomena.

Fundamentalism is not orthodoxy. Webster's New World Dictionary defines orthodox as "conforming to the usual beliefs or established doctrines as, in religion, politics, etc.; approved or conventional" (1978:1004). Fundamentalists claim to ascribe to the "true" essence of a religious doctrine. This is where the common ground between orthodoxy and fundamentalism ends. Fundamentalists are more than orthodox. Their political activism separates them from the orthodox. They are modern while orthodoxy is not (Lawrence, 1989). They are present and future oriented, whereas orthodoxy is past oriented. Fundamentalists use the legitimacy of past ideals to reshape the present and postulate the future. Orthodoxy is otherworldly while fundamentalism is this-worldly.

Fundamentalism is not fanatic. According to Webster, fanatic is "unreasonably enthusiastic, overly zealous . . . a person whose extreme zeal, piety, etc. goes beyond what is reasonable" (1978:505). The important word here is "unreasonable." Fundamentalists are also accused of being irrational, which "implies mental unsoundness" or "the utterly illogical nature of that which is directly contrary to reason" (ibid.:745). Being synonymous, they both imply "bad judgment, willfulness, (and) prejudice" (ibid.:745). The notion of rationalism is at the heart of the fundamentalism. For Barr, Protestant fundamentalism is rational and based on reason (1981). But he is in a minority. The hegemony of positivism, and its associated notion of equating science with reason and knowledge, degrades other forms of information. As Lawrence aptly puts it:

> Technological discoveries, with their accent on commercial discovery and quantitative (not qualitative) output, emphasize reliance on only one kind of reason. A limited appreciation of reason was not common to all scientists, but it became the popular understanding of the

reason=common sense=usefulness=science seriatim equation. . . . (1989:56)

Irrational means fanatic and dangerous. The Scopes trial is often cited as an example of the fanatic and irrational nature of Protestant fundamentalism. In the spring of 1993, when a group of Muslim men were accused of bombing the World Trade Center in New York City, all the images associated with fanatical, irrational, and dangerous were conjured up in the public mind.

It is not regressive. When the Islamic revolution took place in Iran, many observers warned that Iran was going back in time, rejecting the achievements of modernization and Westernization. Given the fundamentalists' claim to the original doctrine, particularly in civil and family regulations, this may seem justified. The Muslims' return to *Shariat* and their rhetoric on gender segregation, and the Protestants' call for uniting God and country and rejection of the women's movement, reinforce such a description (Falwell, 1980; Chandler, 1984). It is this feature of fundamentalism that leads to its clash with modernism. For now, I will suggest that fundamentalism is selectively regressive and thus selective in its response to modernism.

After constructing a conceptual boundary for any fluid notion, we set ourselves up to be questioned and face deconstruction. For the purpose of this research, I will draw some loose boundaries around the notion of fundamentalism.

It is contemporary. It is a response to present-day issues. Marty suggests that "Fundamentalism occurs on the soil of traditional cultures" (1992:18). Lawrence maintains that fundamentalism has "historical antecedence" (1989:100). This historical tradition is recast to address "today" and now. Fundamentalists dwell on the past as long as it is relevant to the present. Their historical discourse is not merely intended to set the record straight; it is geared toward correcting the present deviation from the true path. The Protestant fundamentalists, by holding true that the Bible is the word of God and is inerrant, are hastening its application to the present. The five fundamentals that are considered nonnegotiable by Protestant fundamentalists free the supporters from intellectual debate to engage in activism.

It is active. This is often cited as the hallmark of fundamentalism as compared to previous reawakening or revivalist movements. Compared to the quietism or retreatism of previous trends, fundamentalists are active and aggressive. After the Scopes trial in America, evangelicals retreated from public life and into the churches (Chandler, 1984; Speer, 1984). Similarly, in the Middle East, facing aggressive and militant secular governments, religious leaders who had participated in independence movements across the region retreated into the mosques and their *Madreseh* (theological centers). The new wave senses a dire challenge to its core and thus actively seeks power to halt the attack and reclaim its past glory.

It is a response to a threat. Whether actual or perceived, fundamentalists respond to an assault on their ideal normative system. Fundamentalists perceive their position as being a minority under attack from outside forces. Marty suggests that "threats may come from within, as when someone in a group turns innovator, experimenter, or adapter" (1992:19). For the fundamentalists, however, these revisionists are seen as lackeys of the enemy, duped or co-opted by the outsiders, not as true believers. An insider who revisits the core principles could not have been an insider but a fake.

The threat is defined in anti-faith terms, for example, secular humanism, imperialism, and Westernization (Caplan, 1987; Zubaida, 1987). The threat has access to the political apparatus and consequently to power. This power is the tool of evil and is doing Satan's work. Lawrence points out that fundamentalists are advocates of a pure minority viewpoint. "Even when the remnant/vanguard seizes political power, and seems to become the majority, as happened in Iran in 1979, they continue to perceive and project themselves as a minority" (1989:100). The point here is that fundamentalism, especially Islamic fundamentalism, is anti-Western and anti-imperialistic. This global focus of the movement allows it to perceive itself as under attack, surrounded, and a minority. While the Protestant fundamentalists are concerned with reviving American greatness, Islamic fundamentalists are focused on fighting

American hegemony, thus the attack on American establishments in America and abroad.

It rejects skepticism. For the fundamentalist, ideology and
group membership come as a package, in toto. Participants are
strongly discouraged to dismantle the package and pick and
choose parts that appeal to their individual views. Since the
decision is between God and evil, there is no room for
compromise and doubters. To maintain group solidarity,
fundamentalists resort to labeling, eternal damnation,
psychological isolation, and the use of force. A devoted member
of the Assemblies of God told the author that when she missed a
Wednesday night service to care for a sick child, the pastor told
her, "We choose our action and the Lord chooses our
punishment."

The last two features of the group are closely interrelated.
The more a fundamentalist group feels isolated and threatened,
the stronger is the emphasis on in-group association and loyalty.
Similarly, these two features are related to the next one, namely
boundary maintenance.

To separate the in-group from the out-group,
**fundamentalists develop a complicated behavioral and
communication code** to make identification simple. These codes
serve to locate the in-group and warn the out-group.

In terms of behavior, the members may practice
identifying rituals, use dress codes and insignia, engage in body
rituals (i.e., growing beards among Muslim men and speaking in
tongues among the Protestants), etc. Douglas (1970) suggests
that the more closed a group's ideology, the more bodily control
it exerts over its members. Fundamentalists, like any other
group, develop their own argot. Some extreme antiabortion
fundamentalists in America insist on calling family planning
clinics "abortion mills." This is intended to abhor outsiders while
exposing them to the group's agenda. Stoning adulterers or
carrying a dead fetus to a family planning center are public acts
of boundary maintenance.

As a consequence of the above features, **fundamentalists
are exclusionary groups.** They do not practice an open-door
membership policy. In many groups, membership requires an
ascribed characteristic, such as in the Khalsa movement among

the Sikh, Haredim among Jews, and Baptist fundamentalism among white Americans. While the fundamentalist group may align itself temporarily with an outside group for political or military exigencies, for example, Baptists and Catholics against abortion, they do not recruit among the outsiders. This is perhaps the most visible feature of fundamentalism, which leads to labels like prejudice, intolerance, and racism

      Next, I will address the regressive nature of fundamentalism.

A Gendered Explanation

While permeating all aspects of social life and organizations, fundamentalist movements have paid more attention to politics and family. In other words, these areas have been the main target of religious fundamentalists to reformulate and reorganize. Following the above description, two issues demand particular attention with regard to this research:

> What is a religious fundamentalist vision of social order? Is it ordained by God or maintained by citizens? How does this relate to the separation of God as a source of sacred power and the state as a source of secular power?
>
> Is the family a microcosm of this larger ordained system? Is then the father's authority ordained by God? How does this affect sex roles in the society?

      Fundamentalist discourse revolves around three interconnected circles of faith, family, and state. Other variants of similar combinations have been suggested (see Bradley and Khor, 1993). These fluid circuits overlap, change, and constantly create a new configuration. They are dynamic, and none can survive in isolation. Faith provides the ideological foundation for mobilization. Mccarthy Brown suggests that fundamentalism is the "religion of the stressed and the disoriented" (1994:175). If so, religion provides direction for protestation, rebellion, and, if successful, premises for restructuring. The state should be the manifestation of ordained power. Finally, family is the building block of a godly society, structured after a divine formula.

These circles operate in a circumfluent fashion. Faith provides the instruction, the state the tools, and the family the building foundation for a godly system. Vigilance is required in all three circles, particularly the family because the family's anomie will spread rapidly to other social institutions and foster universal moral decay.

Women, being the central figure of the family, bear the brunt of holding the family together, preserving morality, and safeguarding continuity. Since they cannot be trusted to do this on their own wits or wills, mechanisms are in place to safeguard their morality and consequently the faith. Whereas self-sacrificing and submissive women, such as Mary or Fatimah, were crucial for the perfect societies of the past, modernity has fostered selfishness in women, which in turn has led the society to moral decadence.

A configuration of these circles cast in private/public dimensions presents a holistic system of faith, family, and state operating in a bi-spheric cosmos. None is exclusively concerned with one domain. As indicated in chapter 1, the state regulates the private aspects of family relations and draws its legitimacy from the enforcement of the ordained. In return, the family provides the state with a supportive constituency. It is the state's responsibility to safeguard the family against incursion of foreign values and practices. By doing so, it protects the faith and, as a consequence, safeguards its right to rule.

One needs to envision a continuously dynamic configuration of the circles. The three circles are always engaged, otherwise the system would disintegrate. They often overlap, may align in a synchronized fashion, or one may eclipse the other two. Fundamentalists start by suggesting that the three centers are disengaged, with the family and the state operating in a self-serving manner devoid of the ordained laws.

The debate about fundamentalism as being modern or anti-modern (see Barr 1981; Lawrence 1989; and Bruce 1992) ignores the point that fundamentalism can be, and is, both. When it concerns itself with the public domain—the economy and polity—fundamentalism is modern; when it looks toward the private domain—the family and women's status—fundamentalism is anti-modern or regressive.

The gendered vision of fundamentalism is more apparent in the overlapping areas. The double life of fundamentalism, cooperating and modern at the public level and traditional at the private level, is reflected in these interlocking circles, as shown in figure 2.1. Woman's realm is the family, or the C circle. Her involvement in the other domains of A and B should be an extension of her familial obligations. Accordingly, women's engagement in the two large circles of A and B, outside the overlaps and independent of the family, is strongly discouraged.

Ideally, the fundamentalists envision an eclipse of the other two circles by faith, regulating as well as conducting the affairs of state and family. In this case, the area denoted by d will be expanded under supremacy of the faith. In reality, however, fundamentalists strive to expand the c area and swallow family as much as possible. This configuration will reduce the b area and basically will leave faith and state to vie for managing social organization and formulating the normative order. In contrast, secularism will vie for subsuming faith under the state.

FIGURE 2.1 INTERLOCKING RELATIONSHIP
BETWEEN STATE, FAITH, AND FAMILY

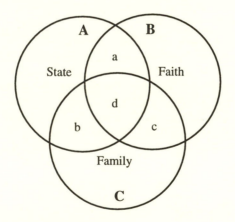

a: nuclear disarmament or Jihad;
b: taxation;
c: sexual obligations or family structure;
d: education, reproduction, or child custody.

The discourse between religion and modernism is marred by patriarchy. Although cast in universal terms, science and religion are gendered entities, which detracts from their universal application. Comte "equated religion with childhood, philosophy and science with adulthood" (in Lawrence, 1989:11). Such a projection conveys a distorted image of historical trends. When religion, philosophy, and science emerged, their battle for dominion took place in a male-centered universe of discourse. These are conceptual stages in the life of a male entity, not a female entity.

The battle between modernism and fundamentalism demands a gendered explanation. We have drawn some delineating lines around what is fundamentalism. Modernism itself is one of those catchall cultural constructs that as soon as formulated begs for deconstruction. Generally speaking, modernism is associated with the supremacy of science, and the latter is closely linked with positivism, which holds as true the supremacy of reason over faith, observation over judgment, and detachment over passion.

According to Lawrence:

> Modernism is the search for individual autonomy driven by a set of socially coded values emphasizing change over continuity, quantity over quality; efficient production, power, and profit over sympathy for traditional values or vocations, in both public and private spheres. At its utopian extreme, it enthrones one economic strategy, consumer oriented capitalism, as the surest means to technological progress that will also eliminate social unrest and physical discomfort. (1989:27)

The idea that modernism penetrates all areas of social life is noted by others. According to Bruce:

> [T]he basic assumptions that inform modern industrial production—that all complex objects and procedures can be reduced to repeatable acts and replaceable components, that nothing is more than the sum of its parts, that everything can be measured and calculated, that nothing is sacred and that everything can be improved—cannot be confined to the world of work. The formal rationality

which dominates that sphere gradually invades all other
areas of social action. (1992:63)

Fundamentalism is also defined as an all-encompassing
social phenomenon responding to and rejecting modernism. For
Lawrence, "fundamentalism is the affirmation of religious
authority as holistic and absolute. . . . " (1989:27). When two
hegemonic forces clash for dominion over formulation of social
order and definition of legitimate citizenry, the battlefield is not
evenly spread. Each suffers from a weak point that allows the
other to prod and attack. In the battle between fundamentalism
and modernism, this juncture is in the private domain.

These two forces are both pervasive and hegemonic.
Modernism, in particular, is more predominant and inclusive. It
permeates all aspects of social life, though unevenly. Its material
dimension is more pervasive and more easily adopted than its
normative system—modern values and norms. The lag between
material adaptation and cultural transformation is more
prominent in the private domain, which is the weak link in the
modernization process.

Modernism as a whole stage—both in terms of material
products and the normative order—is more readily institutionalized in the public than in the private sphere. Peripheral and
subperipheral areas are incorporated into the capitalist world
economy and produce for the capitalist world market. World
system participation leaves very little unchanged in the
economies of even the most remote societies. Research on the
world-system incorporation indicate that economical and
political structures of the participating societies change during
and after incorporation (Dos Santos, 1970; Chase-Dunn, 1975,
1983; Evans, 1979). World system participation also affects the
structure of the household. Women find employment in the
formal labor market and access new products.

New technology, when available and affordable, mod-
ernizes the household even in traditional societies. However, the
value system that made these new inventions and that regulates
their utilization is either blocked or untiringly controlled. For
instance, the new communication technology produces a major
headache for what Riesebordt (1993) calls radical patriarchal
states or organizations. Video players, recorders or cameras, and

satellite technology that transfer modern and Western values into remote areas pose an unending challenge to social agencies committed to safeguarding some "unsoiled" tradition. Meanwhile, these agencies want and need the same technologies to reinforce the tradition, promote their ideology, and learn about others' agendas. In sum, modernism is more public than private. It promotes individual choice, change over continuity, and homogenization of the population. But it fails to deliver them evenly in both social spheres of life.

Change, when it comes to women's domain, is much slower than when it comes to men's. It takes modernizing and modern societies longer to grant women the franchise, offer them education, employ them in the public sector, provide them with health care, and guarantee their individual civil and human rights. It is not surprising, then, that in 1993 the United Nations for the first time considered rape as a war crime. In any society, areas can be easily identified in which women need to match men's gain. Women have to fight twice to gain the same rights as men: the first time for everyone's rights (which means men's rights), and then a second time to obtain the same rights for themselves. Examples can be found in the independence movements of various kinds. Women are mobilized to further the cause of national independence and are then told not to push too hard for their own rights, which may derail the movement. They are told to wait, that it is too early.

Bruce (1987:58) suggests that modernism offers alternatives. One needs to add a qualifier: mostly in the public domain. Women's alternatives are late in coming, limited in scope, and lower in social value. As indicated earlier, women's individual autonomy is delayed and granted piecemeal, and even then it lacks the intensity and enforcement of men's autonomy.

Since modernism penetrates the private domain slowly and marginally, fundamentalism can root there and have a stronger claim. Fundamentalism is more private than public. Where modernism is weak, fundamentalism is strong. In the public domain, fundamentalism gives more to modernism in order to further its own hegemonic goals.

"Fundamentalists seek authority" (Marty, 1992:20). Their claim to pursuing authority is toward an end: dominion of their faith. To this end (access to authority and its safeguard), they must and do utilize modern technology and social organizations. When in power, as in America in the 1980s and presently in Iran, they do not reshape the state apparatus according to the original authority structure. The Islamic Republic doubled the number of government ministries compared to the Shah's period. The New Christian Right (NCR) reinvented capitalism as a biblical premise (Falwell, 1980; Rubenstein, 1986).

Fundamentalists' thirst for new technology, particularly means of force, is well noted (Rubenstein, 1986; Marty, 1992). It is their selection and rationalization that at times are dumbfounding. The NCR advocated the use of nuclear bombs and Star Wars weaponry, but it opposes RU40 (the abortion pill). In the Islamic Republic, street posters advertise video players, though owning one is illegal. The rationalization fails one, unless the dualistic nature of modernism and fundamentalism is recognized. To revitalize the economy, the Rafsanjani government promotes free-market capitalism, but it cannot convince its radical colleagues in the *Majles* (the parliament) to relax regulation of private consumption. Video tapes, produced in America and watched in homes, promulgate the dreaded Western values; yet, advertising them earns the city and government revenue.

Let us digress here and briefly review Muslims' views of modernism. For Muslims, modernism is associated with Westernization and colonialism and thus is more suspected and resisted. Moghadam suggests that "Islamist movements are a product of the contradictions of transition and modernization; they also result from the North-South contention. What is unclear is whether they impede or accelerate the transition to modernity" (1993:138). Realizing they cannot revamp modernization, Muslims struggle to adapt it on a per-need basis. After independence, many Middle Eastern countries adopted available Western models—open-door capitalism or socialism—and aligned themselves with one super power (Zubaida, 1987; Saiedi, 1986). Nasser preferred socialism and the Shah adopted capitalism. Here we will refrain from debating the issue of free choice in the selection process. Whatever the mechanism of adoption, the results were less than satisfactory. Rampant poverty and unemployment, increasing population, military defeats (whether a country was directly involved or not), and other seemingly insurmountable problems have left the people and the intelligentsia searching for an alternative (Ayubi, 1980; Esposito, 1992).

Among the Middle Easterners, as among other third world people or exploited minorities of Western societies, the legacy of colonialism and the experience of imperialism have left a deep sense of powerlessness and other-blaming. The failure of the Nasserites or the Pahlavis is due to the superpowers' intervention or to Western ways. There are few inward-looking collective efforts, except partly for the fundamentalists.

Muslim fundamentalists, too, place the blame for the current crisis in the region at the door of the West, which they also blame for the corruption of the Islamic ethos. They are looking inward insofar as calling for a return to the Islamic ways and expressing disdain for the Western methods. Since Westernization and modernization in the form of large government bureaucracies, new transportation, modern health care, or modern ideas about government by representation cannot be completely eradicated, the goal is selective adaptation of modernism. What is compatible with Islam will stay; what is not has to go.

It is in this selective adaptation of modernism to Islam that the private domain is singled out to be the bastion of the incorruptible Islam. Fundamentalists experiment with Islamic economy and the government of the *Ulamma* (religious leaders). Some of these are pure window dressing, some are more genuine (Saiedi, 1986). Despite their rhetoric, they gradually go to the World Bank and ask for loans, accept the bank's preconditions, and pay the interest fees. Modernization in the public domain is cantankerous and unyielding.

But the private domain is all together a different story. Muslim fundamentalists sense a free hand in the protection of their household from the undesirable influences of Westernization and modernization. An extreme case is the resistance of Afghan men to education and employment of women

(Moghadam, 1992). Fundamentalists in other countries show varying degrees of resistance to the modernization of the private domain. In chapter 6, we will discuss how the Islamic Republic's militancy has adapted to practical considerations and has recognized modernization of women's status in some areas.

The clash of the fundamentalists with modernism is intended not to eradicate the latter but rather to control it. In this, fundamentalists are not alone. Liberal intellectuals debate the utility of unbridled modernism, particularly its technological growth. As Weber predicted, modernism has left a portion of humanity well fed and cared for but naked and isolated (Weber, 1946). The rage of secularism has severed our ties with the cosmos through a God, at the same time failing to provide as convincing and reassuring a link as a God.

Here we come back again to the issue of regression. To label fundamentalists as regressive can be misleading. It is mostly in the family issues that they hold fast to traditional practices, but when it comes to politico-economic structure, they give in little to the past. It is this interplay between fundamentalism and modernism that has escaped the attention of scholars as well as the public's mind. Recognizing the gendered nature of these phenomena allows one to conjure up a clearer picture of their shapes as they span the social landscape.

The interaction between these recalcitrant forces shapes the social definition of woman. Until recently, most of their discourse occurred in the male domain. More and more women participate and influence the contour of their interaction. This study proposes to debate these issues with women themselves. The author has had a unique opportunity to observe two distinct fundamentalist trends. During the past eleven years, I have been stationed at a Midwestern town in America with strong fundamentalist sentiment. Four Bible colleges and the headquarters for the Assemblies of God inform the texture of public opinion in the town. I have had conversations with women and men who strongly support fundamentalist premises and those who vehemently oppose them. Meanwhile, being a native of Iran, I have maintained close contact with that country and its middle-class urban groups. Going back and forth between the two societies provided irresistible intellectual challenges.

During this time, Iran constituted an Islamic Republic, defended and fought an eight-year war with Iraq, and initiated an aggressive campaign to remove the residue of modernization from the family and women's status. At the same time in the United States, Protestant fundamentalists managed to propel an unlikely candidate to the presidency and maintained a strong presence in the public arena. The interaction between American conservatism and Iranian fundamentalism haunted three American administrations, and the juxtaposition continues.

Meanwhile, similar fundamentalist trends in other parts of the world, particularly in the Middle East, were destroying old alliances and challenging established assumptions. Fundamentalist movements from India to Algeria vie for attention. Modernized Egypt is struggling with one of these movements. There, fundamentalist groups are set to replace a secular, Western-oriented government with an Islamic one. Women's rights and roles are central to all of these cases. Women themselves are involved in the centrifugal forces, pro and con.

I was propelled by scientific curiosity and personal desire to gauge women's attitude toward these trends. A cross-cultural study was clearly the only plausible way. Iran is a third world country in which the fundamentalists have managed the forces of a national revolution to successfully enthrone an Islamic state. Despite daunting adversities, the Islamic Republic has managed to survive and thrive. In the United States of America, the fundamentalists managed to place presidents friendly to their cause in the White House. There, too, despite some setbacks and adverse publicity surrounding television evangelists, the fundamentalists are forming strong grass roots programs. Egypt is another Muslim third world country in which a resilient fundamentalist movement is bent on changing the course of postindependence Egypt. They utilize both peaceful means and violent tactics in their campaign.

These three countries provide a diversity of social scales for modernization, industrialization, and the evolution of fundamentalist movements. Comparing them is a task with tantalizing similarities and daunting disparities. What do women say about the juxtaposition of modernism and fundamentalism? The next four chapters deal with this question.

CHAPTER THREE

American Women's Stand on the New Christian Right

Introduction

This chapter focuses on American women's perception of their changing role and place due to the rise of religious fundamentalism and their participation in the New Christian Right movement. The NCR has challenged the legitimacy of feminist causes and even the desirability of some of their achievements, like legalized abortion. This movement has reasserted motherhood and homemaking as women's primary functions and has rejected the equalitarian agenda of the women's movement. Based on Western Christian ideology, the NCR claims that men and women have different capacities, which, accordingly, dictate their social functions. Any legislation ignoring these differences is harmful to women and family.

From its inception, women have participated in this movement, which in turn has redefined aspects of their social status. This chapter measures the extent of women's support for the NCR's agenda. A survey of midwestern women measures the effect of the movement on women's perception of their "proper" role and place, their relation to power at home and in the society, and their degree of feminist consciousness. Furthermore, women's attitude toward the social issues of abortion, gambling, pornography, and homosexual rights are measured. Finally, evidence of a gender gap is examined.

Historical Background of the New Christian Right

During the 1960s, Americans challenged many established patterns of racial, ethnic, gender, and class relations. The familiar mores in personal and social affairs became unacceptable. Government's authority to engage in military and covert operations in other countries in the name of the people was questioned. The old moral order was rebuked, and people searched for a new normative system. The new moral order sought a remaking of traditional sex roles and reformulation of the conservative agenda to match new realities.

By the mid-1970s, various social movements had redefined the American value system and changed aspects of social structure. During this period, class boundaries also shifted, leading to an upward mobility of a segment of the lower classes. A consequence of these changes was a rising tide of political conservatism and religious fundamentalism. Among the features of this trend are the prominence of Christianity, laissez-faire economy, strong militarism, campaign against big government, and patriotism (Klatch, 1987; Beck, 1992). The movement is known as the New Christian Right mostly because it rejects the passivity of the old religious establishment and promotes political activism of religious groups and organizations.[1] The conservative trend is multidimensional. A summary of the NCR's approach to the economy, government, and family provides an overview of these trends.

Economy

The early organizers of the New Christian Right were primarily concerned with the spread of communism and the intrusion of the welfare state. However, they realized that economic issues lack mass appeal. In order to mobilize public support, they forged a coalition with evangelicals and fundamentalists and championed conservative social causes as well. Under the banner of opposition to the Equal Rights Amendment, abortion, homosexual rights, and related causes, the leaders of the New Christian Right successfully rallied support for a conservative economic agenda.

Durham (1985:184), referring to a report in the *Conservative Digest*, suggests that "social issues . . . such as abortion, pornography, and crime were central to the movement's growth, not because they were the most important issues per se, but because 'at least for the present' they were what people cared about." He also quotes a leader of the New Christian Right who had said "We talk about issues that people care about like gun control, abortion, taxes and crime. Yes, they are emotional issues, but that's better than talking about capital formation."

New Christian Right advocates believe that capitalism is a religiously ordained economic system of production (Zewer, 1984; Klatch, 1987:23). "The free enterprise system is clearly outlined in the Book of Proverbs in the Bible. Jesus Christ made it clear that the work ethic was a part of the Plan for Man. Ownership of property is Biblical. Competition in business is Biblical. Ambitious and successful business management is clearly outlined as a part of God's Plan for His people" (Falwell, 1980:13). The Christian ethic and capitalism have made America a unique world power and any tampering with this combination is a deviation from the divine order. Programs such as welfare are perceived to weaken the work ethic, increase the tax burden of working people, and benefit those who do not work (Gilder, 1981). Furthermore, social assistance programs make the government a social equalizer, which is equivalent to socialism and thus undesirable (Beck, 1992). These programs are more effective when they are handled by charitable organizations and only when they help the "true needy."

Government regulations of industry, conservation measures, and even foreign aid are seen to have a stifling effect on the economy (Exter and Barber, 1986). The NCR is also distrustful of big business, particularly multinational corporations. The hands-off approach to business mostly applies to small businesses and does not concern the multinational corporations.

Big Government

A promise of the Reagan campaign was to take government off people's backs. This and similar statements underline the undesirability of government intervention in social arenas. At the family level, government, by making child care tax deductible, encourages working mothers. This policy encourages mothers of young children to seek jobs outside the home, which is detrimental to the nuclear family (Gilder, 1981). In addition to raising the tax burden of other citizens, this action goes against the Christian vision of the family, with mother as homemaker. It removes parental authority and opens the door to state supervision of children. Abbott and Wallace maintain that the White House Conference on Families and "Jimmy Carter's vision of the role of government in supporting and sustaining families" further intensified the NCR's campaign against big government (1992:44).

Another example of big government's intrusion occurs through public education. Big government, with its vast apparatus of the public school system, promotes secular humanism. Separation of church and state has given free rein to secular humanists to promote their agenda of sex education, cultural relativism, evolution, and acceptance of alternative life styles. Heinz (1983:140) suggests that the New Christian Right sees this as leaving education devoid of any religious legitimacy. Furthermore, busing and control over textbook selection and curriculum in schools are seen as the federal government's involvement in family affairs and usurpation of parental authority.

The Equal Rights Amendment (ERA) was condemned for the same reasons. Under the banner of Christian morality, various factions of the New Christian Right forged a coalition with some of the Old Right groups to defeat the ERA. It was seen as another example of the federal government's intrusion into business and family. Its passage, it was argued, would promote a wide range of liberal causes, from unisex toilets and homosexual marriage to the drafting of women into the military. As Phyllis Schlafly, the spokeswoman for the STOP-ERA campaign, stated, "This legislative history makes it crystal clear that ERA will subject women to absolutely equal treatment in and by the military" (1981:104). She then continues, "Equality in the military is unfair to everyone, the serviceman, the service-woman, and the American people who are paying the cost" (ibid.:110).

Equally undesirable is the federal government's involvement in family planning. Legalized abortion has come to symbolize the New Christian Right's perception of the immorality of the liberals, feminists, and big government. These forces are seen as to be responsible for the social ills gripping the American family and society.

Family

The NCR's polemic is imbued with family as the symbol of Christianity and God. Under the banner of "Christian Family," the New Christian Right addresses a wide range of issues from abortion and sex education to strong defense, anti-gun-control legislation, and other conservative causes (Heinz, 1983). Conover and Gray (1983:77) quote Gasper, who states:

> The media have attempted to erroneously paint the Pro-Family Movement as being only anti-abortion and anti-ERA. The Pro-Family Movement is a broad-based coalition of social conservatives who recognize the value of person, the importance of the family, the rights and responsibility of parents, and the importance of restricting government so that there can be personal freedom.

Conover and Gray show how the New Christian Right and conservative groups have emphasized family in their organizational titles, such as "Pro-Family United," "American Family Institute," and "International Federation for Family Life Protection" (1983:211–14). Family is the NCR's launching pad for a comprehensive sociopolitical agenda that includes opposition to the following:

Equal Rights Amendment

Opposition to ERA was the single issue that helped to bring together other single-issue groups of the New Christian Right for future campaigns. The leaders of the anti-ERA coalition saw it as another attempt by the federal government to expand its authority at the cost of state governments. Business, particularly small businesses, were afraid of unforeseen consequences of the amendment, such as maternity benefits, parental leave, and comparable worth pay. To mobilize mass opposition, anti-ERA leaders, such as Phyllis Schlafly, cast their campaign in terms of moral values. Passage of the amendment, it was claimed, would lead to antifamily legislation, legalization of homosexual marriage, denigration of women's traditional roles, and drafting of women into the military (Boles, 1979; Mansbridge, 1986). Phyllis Schlafly states:

> ERA will force upon us the rigid, unisex, gender-free mandate demanded by the women's liberation movement, and it will transfer the power to apply this mandate to the federal government and the federal courts, where average citizens have no control. (1981:141)

Homosexual Rights

Homosexuality, especially any legitimation of the relationship, rallies various NCR groups. It also helps the movement to attract new constituencies who may not otherwise sympathize with the movement. Anti-ERA groups effectively utilized gay/lesbian participation in Pro-ERA rallies to attract noncommitted observers (Mansbridge, 1986). Warning against ERA, Schlafly states, "Depending on the ultimate interpretation of the rule that bars treating 'persons differently on the basis of sex,' the HEW regulation may even prohibit schools and colleges from refusing to admit prostitutes, homosexuals, and lesbians"[2] (1981:135). Indeed, it has proven to be an effective banner under which the New Christian Right can rally against any issue.

Legalized Abortion

The most effective and the most controversial single issue of the NCR since the ERA is women's right to legalized abortion. When ERA was being ratified in state assemblies, antiabortion groups postponed their fight and rallied to defeat ERA first. Since then, with the help of new groups, the NCR has turned abortion into the most potent political issue. To begin with, the group appropriated pro-life as a positive title and tries to portray the pro-choice coalition as antilife.

Abortion has several conceptual and practical implications for the "Christian Family" as it is perceived by the New Christian Right: (1) It challenges the basic premise of the patriarchal family, which is man's authority over woman's body. (2) It allows woman to make unilateral decisions about her own body and its reproductive power. (3) Consequently, like ERA, abortion separates woman's identity from the family and regards her as an autonomous individual. Woman's distinct identity is perceived by men and women to be threatening to the preservation of the family unit. If women seek to realize their true "selves" outside the family—men's prerogative—the very structure of the unit is affected. (4) It reduces man's power over the whole unit by placing woman in charge of the family size. (5) Finally, abortion undermines the Christian doctrine of human sexuality, which allows sex for reproduction rather than for pleasure.[3] Contraceptives or abortion, which can hamper reproduction or make the sexual act only for pleasure, can lead to moral decay and eventually destroy the basic fabric of the "Christian Family." Women who oppose abortion and ERA do so for the sake of preserving the nuclear family. They are more likely to support women's rights within the family, such as the right to divorce or maternity benefits, than individualistic rights.

Feminism

Feminism was the focal point around which all anti-God and antifamily arguments rested (Pollack Petchesky, 1981; Dworkin, 1982). Feminism is a multifaceted concept that often generates strong reaction from listeners. Beginning with the rise of religious fundamentalism and the increased power of the NCR, this response has become increasingly negative. Offen (1988:136) traces the history of the concept to two forms of feminism: relational and individualistic.[4] Relational feminism

> emphasized women's right as "women" (defined principally by their childbearing and/or nurturing capacities) in relation to men. It insisted on women's distinctive contributions in these roles to the border

society.... By contrast, the individualist feminist tradition
of argumentation emphasized more abstract concepts of
individual human rights and celebrated the quest for
personal independence (or autonomy) in all aspects of life,
while down playing ... sex-linked qualities and
contributions, including childbearing and its attendant
responsibilities.

Individualistic feminism allows the single woman "an
independent, non-family based existence" (ibid.:137), which
consequently questions the legitimacy of women's existence in
relation to men, children, and family. Motherhood and
homemaking functions of women are fundamentally community
based. They ground women's status solidly in the family and in
relation to other roles in that domain. It is also through these
functions that women's roles in society are formulated. In the
family and society, woman's nurturing capacity defines her
existence in terms of services that she provides for others. If this
"nurturing capacity" is attributed to a natural or divine source,
then the concomitant roles are "given" and not "chosen."

Individualistic feminism, in order to survive, needs to
question, if not reject, this view of woman's nature. As a consequence, it has to question all gender-based social responsibilities
and attributes. Thus, it can be easily misinterpreted as being antifamily. This is how the New Christian Right perceives the
women's movement of the 1970s as antifamily, antiwomen, anti-
God, and selfish. "The woman in the Garden of Eden freely
decided to tamper with God's order and ignore His rules. She
decided to do things her own way, independent of God's com-
mandment. She even persuaded the man to join her in
'liberation' from God's Law. Sin thus entered the world, bringing
fear, sickness, pain, anger, hatred, danger, violence, and all va-
rieties of ugliness" (Schlafly, 1981:14).

This form of feminism is antifamily by supporting
abortion. It is antiwomen by defining motherhood and
homemaking as matters of choice rather than as God-given and
"natural" functions. As a consequence, it is anti-God—by
questioning the ordained structure of the nuclear patriarchal
family and by supporting women's right to abortion. Finally, it is
selfish because it calls for women's independent identity in the

public domain, distinct and separate from her roles in the private domain.

The last objective of the feminists has led to the accusation that they "behave like men and wish to be treated like men." This has two ramifications as far as the NCR is concerned. One, as Klatch indicates, is that when women stop being altruistic the result is "total masculinization of the world" (1987:129). Second, women's independent identity in the public domain disturbs the structure of the "Christian Family" in the private domain, which is God, Man, and Woman. Indeed, an independent public identity fosters demand for an equalitarian relationship in the private domain, against the hierarchical order of the family. These and other issues alienated a large number of women whose self-identity was grounded on their nurturing roles and pushed them into the NCR's camp.

The women leaders of the NCR reasserted woman's innate need for nurturing, as Phyllis Schlafly states, "so that [it] doesn't well up inside her and cause psychological frustration" (1981:24). According to Elliot, "every normal woman is equipped to be a mother . . . motherhood, in a deeper sense, is essence of womanhood" (1976:62). Therefore, feminists are not normal women and are antiwomen.

Now, in hindsight, it is easy to see why feminism is perceived as antiwomen. Feminists raised the issue of self-realization and achieving personal fulfillment through nontraditional channels. While they were claiming woman's legitimate place in the public domain, they were perceived as denigrating her role in the private domain. NCR advocates believe that motherhood and homemaking are women's most worthy endeavors and should be considered as such.

Features of the Christian Family

For the NCR, family is the foundation of a strong and moral America as the world leader. It is viewed as the social institution through which God's will for the individual is implemented. Characteristics of the "Christian Family" include the following:

Religious Ordination

"He made man in his own image, and then for the first time God saw something that was not good. It was not good for the man to be alone. God determined to make a helper fit for him. . . . It was a woman God gave him, a woman 'meet', fit suitable, entirely appropriate for him, made of his very bones and flesh" (Elliot, 1976:20–22). Enshrined in the divine order, the nuclear family places alternative family styles in an unfavorable light. Furthermore, any tampering with the structure or shifting of roles are against God's order. The NCR sees in various social movements of the 1960s, especially the women's movement, the root of the destruction of the family and calls for a return to the "Christian Family." As Pat Robertson states: "We've got to come back to the point of Christian marriage, Christian child care, Christian families" (quoted by Klatch, 1987:136). Such a foundation, then, is seen as an answer to the social evils that have been caused by the promiscuity of the 1960s and the 1970s.

Hierarchy of Power

Founded on scripture, the Christian family has a hierarchical order, in which man assumes the position of power and woman functions as his helper and mate. "For man was not made from woman, but woman from man. Neither was man created for woman, but woman for man" (1 Corinthians 11 in Mahowald, 1983:300). Therefore, she should support his decisions and strive toward his goals (Elliot, 1976:22).

This power inequality has "strong biological reasons (a matter of hormones)" and that is "why the male has always dominated and will continue to be dominant in every society" (Elliot, 1976:58). Men not only excel in physical activities but also have mental talents that are different from women's. Phyllis Schlafly (1981:26) supports this argument by a quote from de Riencourt, who states:

> Women tend more toward conformity than men—which is why they often excel in such disciplines as spelling and punctuation where there is only one correct answer, determined by social authority. Higher intellectual

activities, however, require a mental independence and power of abstraction that they usually lack, not to mention a certain form of aggressive boldness of imagination which can only exist in a sex that is basically aggressive for biological reasons.

Therefore men and women perform specific and non-interchangeable functions within the family.

Sex Roles

Clear sexual division of labor promotes complementary sex roles rather than equalitarian relationship. Man is the "decision maker," the "leader," and the protector of women and children (Falwell, 1980:130). Woman's role is primarily at the domestic environment as mother and homemaker. This view of family rejects the idea of gender equality for gender complementarity. It assumes that the sexes have different physical and psychological makeups suitable for specific social functions. The New Christian Right woman believes that "those very differences provide the key to her success as a person and fulfillment as a woman" (Schlafly, 1981:23).

Gilder, another conservative theorist, reaches the same conclusion through a different path (1974; 1981). For him, it is the man who is weaker, unfocused, and aggressive, while woman is stronger, more intelligent, and talented. The savage man needs woman's taming talent and investment, otherwise he is an unattached predator, dangerous to himself and the society. The notion of complementarity, whether it sees the woman as stronger or weaker, reaches the same conclusion: woman's self-denial and sacrifice, and man's self-centeredness and activism.

It is a mistake to assume that the NCR women are socially isolated. On the contrary, they are active in various aspects of the NCR campaign, working for their favorite political issue. The rise of religious fundamentalism has proposed an agenda for women's roles with two items:

1. One is the redefinition of women's roles in terms of traditional values, that is "the earlier form of dominant wage-earning husband and the full-time homemaking

and church volunteering wife and mother as instituted by God" (Hargrove et al., 1985:125), and most desirable.

2. The second item is the political activism of the NCR woman. She is not only a mother and wife, but a political actor. This is not to say that the traditional women were absolutely apolitical. The major difference is that the New Christian Right women are using established means of political participation, like grass roots organization, lobbying, letter writing, demonstration, etc. Indeed, political activism on behalf of the fundamentalist agenda is accepted and encouraged. Women are expected, are encouraged, and desire to participate to further the political power of agencies that advocate fundamentalist causes, more importantly, for the sake of home and family protection.[5]

Among the fundamentalist organizations sponsored by women of the New Christian Right are Phyllis Schlafly's Eagle Forum, Connie Marshner's National Pro-Family Coalition, the antiabortion organization of Judie Brown called American Life League, and Beverly LaHyes's Concerned Women for America (*Time*, 1985; Paige, 1987; Marshall, 1991).

The fact that women have been leaders and active participants in the NCR movement merits further investigation of the extent to which the NCR has influenced women's attitudes in general. This chapter tests the extent of support for the NCR's agenda among women.

American Women Respond

Through its conventional as well as radical tactics—such as blockade of abortion clinics—the NCR has furthered the cause of the conservatives in all aspects of American life. At the national level, it has helped to elect conservative presidents, senators, and representatives. Presidents Reagan and Bush, by appointing conservative judges, have shifted the Supreme Court's composition, which in turn has revamped many legal achievements of the civil rights and women's movements. The

NCR successfully defeated ERA and is close to having *Roe v. Wade* overturned.

At the social level, liberalism has become an anomaly. Family is exalted, and patriotism is synonymous with religion and Christianity. While sex roles have become more flexible, traditional values of family, home, and country permeate the nomenclature. The percentage of women working outside the home is the highest in American history. Nevertheless, femininity is the password and homemaking and motherhood are respectable options and not "given" functions. This seems to be a synthesis of the women's movement.

The apparent fusion of the NCR's values raises the question:

How widespread is women's support for the New Christian Right causes? There are studies measuring women's attitudes toward abortion, child care, and working mothers (Welch, 1975; Blake, 1980; Barnett and Harris, 1982), but we lack a measure of women's identification with the NCR's depiction of their "proper" role and place.

This study proposes that the religious fundamentalist ideology of the New Christian Right defines women's proper place to be mainly at home and in the private domain, and her proper roles are primarily motherhood and homemaking. Any role that she plays in the public is a continuation of her nurturing and helping functions at home; she is mostly engaged in services to men and children.

Political participation contributes to a sense of empowerment. Thus women, by organizing and working for the conservative political agenda, have an increased sense of empowerment at home and in the society. While they may still hold on to the idea that man is the decision maker at home, they may nevertheless express more willingness to assume power.

While they claim activism on behalf of women's issues, the NCR women declare strong opposition to a feminist agenda (Schlafly, 1981; Ehrenreich, 1983; Klatch, 1987). Most of their opposition is to individualistic feminism. Women's issues that they have been advocating, to some extent, resemble relational feminism. They seek validation of women's traditional roles, both at home and in the public. This furthers their pride in their nurturing functions and helps them to formulate its significance for the society, in various social and political forums. This study proposes to measure women's support for feminist issues of gender equality and group consciousness.

Methodology

A questionnaire with five scales was developed. Two scales deal specifically with woman's role versus her place. Another scale measures women's perception of their power at home and in the society. One scale measures group solidarity and the extent of support for feminist issues. Finally, one scale was developed to measure women's support for social conservative issues and the extent to which they identify with the NCR causes.

Respondents

This survey was administered to a sample of 1,500 residents of southwest Missouri by the Center for Social Research of Southwest Missouri State University. Of the total questionnaires, 330 usable returns were received by the center, which amounts to a return rate of 29 percent. "This response rate compares favorably to other mail-out surveys of the general population done in southwest Missouri" (Hartmann, 1988:2). Of the total sample, 47 percent of the respondents were male. Since women's attitude is the topic of this research, only women respondents (N=171) were used for statistical analysis. Whenever the results were not clear, the male sample was used to check the validity of the items in terms of clarity and ambiguity. A comparison of the two groups was used to explore the existence and the extent of gender gap. The conservative social issues index was tested again in 1989. Comparative analysis will be made.

Results

Table 3.1 presents a summary of the respondents characteristics. The majority are employed and married, between the ages of twenty-five and forty-five, and have a minimum of a high school education. Among the female respondents, 44 percent attended church at least once a week. In sum, the women respondents are young, employed, married, have a minimum of high school education, and live in a metropolitan area.

TABLE 3.1. GENERAL CHARACTERISTICS
OF THE AMERICAN SAMPLE (%)

Employment		Years Employed*		Education		Marital		Age	
Ft	45.8	1-5	7.7	< Hs	5.4	M	59.5	19-24	6.5
Pt	13.1	6-10	20.2	Hs	47.3	S	12.5	25-34	26.2
Hsw	9.5	11-15	18.5	2 Cl	22.2	W	14.3	35-44	22.0
Ret	16.7	16-20	15.5	Cl	13.8	D	13.7	45-54	14.0
Std	3.0	>20	34.5	> Cl	11.4			55-64	10.1
Unem	11.9							65+	18.5

Key: Ft = Full Time , Pt = Part Time, Hsw = Housewife, Ret = Retired,
Std = Student, Unem = Unemployed, Hs = High School, Cl = College,
M=Married, S=Single, W=Widowed, D=Divorced
* Not Including students and housewives.

Church Attendance			Residence	
>	1 Week	20.2	Country	16.7
	1 Week	23.8	< 10,000	14.9
	2 Month	5.4	10,000-100,000	19.6
	1 Month	5.4	> 100,000	43.0
<	1 Month	13.1	Suburb	4.8
	Almost N	30.4		

Key: Almost N = Almost Never.

Feminine and Masculine Functions

A recurring theme in the writings and speeches of NCR leaders, both men and women, is the importance of traditional complementary sex roles for family stability (Falwell, 1980). A scale with five items measured attitude toward women's proper role. Tables 3.2 and 3.3 show the result of descriptive statistics for this index. The first three items are designed to measure women's support for this idea. The first item measures the complementary sex roles within the family, with the male as the breadwinner and woman as the homemaker. This is over-whelmingly rejected by the female respondents.

TABLE 3.2. WOMEN'S FUNCTION INDEX

	Mean	Median	Stdev
1. Men's job to bring money, women's family	3.09	3.0	.90
2. Woman give up her job; interfere with family	2.46	2.0	.90
3. Women should emphasize her job as much as his	2.14	2.0	.87
4. Best occupation for women teaching	3.48	4.0	.60
5. Women have easier life	3.56	4.0	.72

Items two and three counterpoise modern women's dilemma of compelling necessity to choose between family and occupation. If woman's primary function is motherhood, then an outside job should be secondary, and whenever it interferes with the family it should be relinquished (item two). The respondents are clearly divided on this issue, with half of them placing the emphasis on woman's responsibility to her family and the other half placing it on her job. Gerson (1985) postulates that social changes in women's life-style have not followed a singular path. Some have veered toward motherhood, some have veered away from it, while others have opted for domesticity without motherhood. If the respondents are divided on the issue of family responsibilities versus occupational responsibilities, they display more consensus with respect to woman's supportive functions. Item three reaffirms the importance of woman's support for man's occupation: should a woman emphasize her job as much as her husband's? Two-thirds of the respondents agree. Prioritizing between the family and occupation is treacherous, combining the two is heavenly.

TABLE 3.3. WOMEN'S FUNCTION: % DISTRIBUTION

		SA	AS	DS	SD
1.	Men's job to bring money, women's	6.0	18.1	36.7	39.2
	family	16.4	33.9	37.6	12.1
2.	Woman give up her job; interfere with				
	family	25.0	42.7	25.6	6.7
3.	Woman should emphasize her job as				
	much as his		5.5	41.2	53.3
4.	Best occupation for women teaching	3.0	4.2	25.9	66.9
5.	Women have easier life				

Key: SA = Strongly Agree, AS = Agree Somewhat, DS = Disagree Somewhat, SD = Strongly Disagree.

The second issue deals with feminine occupation for women. Phyllis Schlafly indicates that women have a psychological need to "love something alive. . . . This is the reason why women have traditionally gone into teaching and nursing careers. They are doing what comes naturally to the female psyche. The school child or the patient of any age provides an outlet for a woman to express her natural maternal need" (1981:23–4). Question four, which tests this idea by suggesting that the best occupation for women is teaching, is overwhelmingly rejected.

The postwar period generated the myth of homebound woman as mother and homemaker and masculine man as the sole breadwinner (Gerson, 1985). This idea of crystalized sex roles and personalities is more mythical than real. Nevertheless, the NCR claims that the women's movement replaced the clarity of traditional sex roles, and their associated rituals of daily interaction, with the ambiguity of new expectations leading to frustration. Has the rise of the NCR and the impetus to femininity made women's lives easier? Women's response to question five, which addresses the above issue, is: No. While this item does not explore the psychosocial complexities of life satisfaction, its result is in line with other studies' findings (Gerson, 1985).

In sum, the results of this index indicate that despite the rhetoric of the NCR and some popular perceptions, women have not internalized the NCR's idea of a functional duality of sex roles for men and women. While they believe that a woman's job is as important as a man's, they have not resolved the conflict between family responsibilities and career requirements. This issue, however, is very clear for men. Over 60 percent believe that a woman should give up her job when it interferes with her family responsibilities.

TABLE 3.4. WOMEN'S FUNCTION: CORRELATION MATRIX

	1	2	3	4	5
1		.46*	-.37*	.21*	.07
2			-.30*	.24*	.08
3				.11	-.16*
4					.07
5					

* $P = <.05$.

Table 3.4 presents bivariate correlations among the items of this index. Strong bivariate relationships between most items suggest a single underlying construct.

Spatial Distinction

This scale is designed to measure support for spatial separation of the sexes. Tables 3.5 to 3.7 display the results. The nurturing capacity of woman locates her in the private domain and restricts her mobility in the public domain. The leaders of the NCR have reaffirmed the ideal of domesticity for women. The question, then, arises: Do women perceive spatial separation of the sexes? The first question deals with woman's financial independence in relation to her nurturing roles. If a woman's happiness is raising children, then she cannot happily pursue economic activities in the public domain and gain economic independence (Schlafly, 1981). Question six, which asks if financial independence is detrimental to women's happiness, is rejected. While the majority of women reject this idea, the 32 percent who support it are more interesting than those who reject it (table 3.6). A standard deviation of .92 indicates that there is disagreement about this issue (table 3.5). Furthermore, the Christian family of a full-time wife and dominant breadwinner husband assigns financial responsibility to the man. This is inconsistent with a working wife. Therefore, such a man's pride is vested in supporting his family and he dislikes for his wife to work (Gilder, 1981) (item seven). Here again, while the majority rejects this idea, a minority of 35 percent supports it (table 3.6).

TABLE 3.5. WOMEN'S PLACE INDEX

	Mean	Median	Stdev
6. Women's financial independence detrimental to happiness	3.0	3.0	.92
7. Proud husband dislikes wife to work	2.77	3.0	.90
8. High unemployment; women should stay home	3.14	3.0	.97
9. Women's ed suitable roles: mother and housewife*	3.58	4.0	.71

* Girl's education should be suitable for her future roles as mother and housewife.

TABLE 3.6. WOMEN'S PLACE: % DISTRIBUTION

	SA	AS	DS	SD
6. Women's financial independence detrimental to happiness	4.9	26.8	29.9	38.4
7. Proud husband dislikes wife to work	9.1	26.8	41.5	22.6
8. High unemployment, women stay home	9.8	11.7	33.7	44.8
9. Girl's ed suitable roles: mother and housewife	1.8	7.3	21.2	69.7

Key: SA = Strongly Agree, AS = Agree Somewhat, DS = Disagree Somewhat,

SD = Strongly Disagree.

NCR advocates reiterate that women prefer to be homemakers but recognize that some women have to work. Should they work, the nature and function of their work makes it secondary to man's work. According to Gilder (1981), middle-class talented women take away jobs from men who need them more. Thus, women should stay at home at times of high unemployment and open up the job market for men (item eight). This item is strongly rejected. Finally, directing women's education toward future roles as mothers and housewives does not receive support from this sample.

Strong positive bivariate correlations between items of this index (table 3.7) further support the underlying construct of women's position.

TABLE 3.7. WOMEN'S PLACE: CORRELATION MATRIX

	6	7	8	9
6		.08	.17*	.1
7			.37*	.23*
8				.32*
9				

*$P = <.05$.

Generally, the result of this scale indicates that the desirability of traditional sex roles promulgated by the NCR has not convinced a sizable number of women. The above scales fail to show women's support for a separate "proper" place or role for each of the sexes. The primacy of man's job as breadwinner is not recognized. Women do not identify with merely a supporting role as the helper and mate of their husbands. The NCR has accused feminists of selfishness in seeking their legitimate place and independent identity in the public and relinquishing their supportive roles in the family. The results of the above scales suggest that this selfishness is quite widespread.

Relation to Power

The structure of the traditional family is based on a unilateral view of authority. "Wives, submit yourselves unto your husbands, as it is fit in the Lord" (Colossians 3:18–19 in Bullough, 1973:101) ordains this premise. Modern advocates of this idea, such as Connie Marshner, maintain that "the woman may become an equal or chief provider. Nevertheless, the husband is still the head of the family. Accepting his authority may be more of a challenge for the woman to accept in that circumstance, but if traditional values are to be preserved, it must be accepted. What is moral is the fact that the wife accepts her husband's authority" (quoted by Klatch, 1987:146).

A scale with five items measures woman's relation to power in terms of (1) gender differences in power management, (2) familial power management, and (3) allegiance to biblical interpretation of female inferiority.

Tables 3.8 to 3.10 present the results of this scale. Question ten explores women's idea regarding the sexes' ability in power management. The majority reject the idea that men are more capable in handling power. A minority of 34 percent, nevertheless, supports men's superior capacity in power management (table 3.9). As far as family issues are concerned, questions eleven and twelve counterpoise man's authority with woman's control in familial issues. This presents a better understanding of the NCR's support for relational feminism. Father's unilateral right to decide important issues in children's lives is rejected (item eleven), and women do not feel they are the power holders at home. Respondents reject man's ordained authority at home, meanwhile disclaiming any hold on the reins of familial power themselves.

TABLE 3.8. WOMEN'S RELATION TO POWER INDEX

	Mean	Median	Stdev
10. Men more capable to handle power	3.04	3.0	1.01
11. Father import. decision for future children	3.41	4.0	.80
12. Women have real power at home	2.62	3.0	.80
13. Weaker physc = weaker mental/psych*	3.83	4.0	.49
14. No intellec. strength for judiciary/politics†	3.62	4.0	.71

* Women due to their weaker physical structures have weaker mental and psychological capacities.
† Women do not have the mental strength necessary for politics and judiciary.

TABLE 3.9. RELATION TO POWER: % DISTRIBUTION

	SA	AS	DS	SD
10. Men more capable in handling power	7.8	25.9	21.1	45.2
11. Father import. decision for future children	4.2	6.7	33.3	55.8
12. Women have real power at home	9.2	30.1	49.7	11.0
13. Weaker physc = weaker mental/psych	1.2	1.2	11.0	86.6
14. No intellec. strength for judiciary/politics	1.8	7.9	17.1	73.2

Key: SA = Strongly Agree, AS = Agree Somewhat, DS = Disagree Somewhat, SD = Strongly Disagree.

TABLE 3.10. RELATION TO POWER:
CORRELATION MATRIX

	10	11	12	13	14
10		.33*	.22	.30*	.35*
11			.11	.23*	.26*
12				.15*	.16*
13					.57*
14					

* $P = <.05$.

According to the evangelical New Christian Right, the Bible is the actual word of God and is to be taken literally. It is also the indisputable source of social codes of conduct. The Bible contains clear references to the inferior intellectual capacity of women. Like Islam, Western Christianity warns men not to rely on women's judgment. The small number of women public officeholders in America also points to a lack of public trust in women's political savvy, rational judgment, and intellectual power. Items thirteen and fourteen measure women's support for the Christian principle of female subordination, and the result is negative.

In sum, the results indicate a lack of support for sexual differences in power management as well as power inequality in household affairs. The respondents also dispute the Christian basis of female intellectual inferiority.

Feminism

A scale with five items is designated to evaluate (1) women's cognitive recognition of gender equality, (2) its practical implications for family roles, and (3) the degree of their group solidarity. Tables 3.11 to 3.13 display the results of this index.

Question fifteen asks women about equality between the sexes. Fifty-one percent of the respondents somewhat disagree with the statement that women can do anything men can (table 3.12). The next two questions deal with familial equality. Equalitarian relations in sharing the household responsibilities, measured by item sixteen, is strongly supported. Given the notion of complementary talents and potentials of the sexes, as envisioned by the NCR, should girls education be different from boys to foster and enrich these differences? An overwhelming majority rejects any distinction in the education of boys and girls measured by item seventeen.

TABLE 3.11. FEMINISM INDEX

		Mean	Median	Stdev
15.	Women can perform any job men can	2.55	2.0	.84
16.	Fair to expect husband to help with chores	1.56	1.0	.71
17.	Educational materials girls = boys	1.59	1.0	.79
18.	Worst enemies of women other women	2.69	3.0	1.01
19.	Cannot trust a woman with a secret	3.40	4.0	.81

TABLE 3.12. FEMINISM: % DISTRIBUTION

		SA	AS	DS	SD
15.	Women can perform any job men do	9.7	38.8	38.2	13.3
16.	Fair to expect husband to help with chores	53.6	38.6	5.4	2.4
17.	Educational materials girls = boys	55.8	32.7	7.9	3.6
18.	Worst enemies of women other women	14.0	29.3	30.5	26.2
19.	Cannot trust a woman with a secret	3.1	11.0	28.8	57.1

Key: SA = Strongly Agree, AS = Agree Somewhat, DS = Disagree Somewhat,
       SD = Strongly Disagree.

The next two items deal with women's group solidarity. The hostility of the fundamentalist women toward the feminists suggests a lack of trust among women themselves. The activities of antifeminist groups date back to the mid-1800s, when they were fighting the suffragist movement (Marshall, 1991). The NCR's rhetoric accuses feminists of devaluating their traditional functions and disrupting the family structure. As Phyllis Schlafly states; "women liberationists operate as Typhoid Marys carrying a germ called lost identity. . . . As a home wrecker, women's liberation is far in the lead over 'the other man,' 'the other woman,' or 'incompatibility'" (1981:72). In addition to these statements, American folk culture is saturated with statements about lack of trust among women or the feeble nature of women's psyche, which cannot be trusted with secrets. The majority of the respondents reject the idea that women are the worst enemies of each other. But a minority of 43 percent supports it (item eighteen, table 3.12). The fact that a large minority supports this idea means it is worth further consideration. While the NCR might bear some responsibility for this, the myth of the other woman may have historically contributed to this lack of trust. However, women strongly reject the idea they are not trustworthy. Table 3.13 shows the correlation matrix for items of this scale.

TABLE 3.13. FEMINISM: CORRELATION MATRIX

	15	16	17	18	19
15		.13	.35*	-.15	-.24*
16			.25*	-.15	-.24
17				.00	.24*
18					.41*
19					

*$P = <.05$.

Taken together, the result of this scale shows that this sample does not support a general blank statement of equality of the sexes. However, at the practical level, familial equality is strongly supported, and there is a moderate level of group solidarity and collective consciousness measured by items eighteen and nineteen.

The NCR women's organizations have claimed widespread membership poised to defend Christian morality and traditional values (*Time*, 1985; Paige, 1987; Beck, 1992). Challenged by a changing world, the New Christian Right, meanwhile, remains fluid. The result of this study does not support a general reorientation of sex roles. Female domesticity is not women's ideal occupation. Many NCR advocates claim that women's labor force participation is due to financial necessity rather than individual preference. The result confirms that women have not replaced work with family and are troubled in choosing between the two. The notion of separate domains for the sexes receives insignificant support. Overall, the ideal of the domestic environment and nurturing functions for women and the public domain and masculine functions for men is refuted.

In terms of power relations, neither at the abstract level nor at practical family level do respondents accept male superiority. There is also no indication that the trend has been reversed and women reign over the family issues. The biblical interpretation of gender inequality fails to summon women's support, too.

Finally, feminism, as measured here, receives moderate support. Rejecting the absolute equality of the sexes, respondents display some degree of group solidarity. The fact that American women have historically posed on two sides of issues, such as suffrage, ERA, and abortion, might explain some of this mistrust.

Woman and the Conservative Agenda

A scale with five social issues was designed to measure respondents' degree of conservatism. These issues have been on the NCR's agenda from its inception. Women supporters of the movement have taken a stand on these issues. Some are more potent than others. The respondents were told that a hypothetical bill pending in the state legislature would ban legalized abortion and legalized gambling, and would establish school prayers, an antipornography law, and homosexual rights. They chose between five options, ranging from "not interested" to "spending time and money to defeat" the bill (see table 3.14).

To begin with, women's attitude on a ban on legalized abortion is in line with the national data (NORC, 1988). Slightly over half, 50.9 percent, would vote against a bill that bans legalized abortion, 8.6 percent claim no interest in this issue (table 3.14). On the issue of legalized gambling, women are divided, with 20.7 percent having no interest. The majority of women support an antipornography law (68.6 percent) and a law establishing school prayers (59.6 percent). The last item deals with homosexual rights. The majority are against any legitimation of homosexual rights.

The social conservatism index was retested in 1989. A higher rate of return of 489 was associated with higher male respondents. This time, 56.5 percent of the sample were male and 43.5 percent were female. This group was also better educated, employed, and was married. The result remained the same, with minor differences. With respect to abortion, the interest rose by about 4 percent (table 3.14). The result of 1989 was after the Supreme Court ruling in the case of Webster versus Reproductive Health Services, which may account for the increased interest in this issue. The majority nevertheless supports legalized abortion, with a slight increase of about 3 percent. Over-all, the trend to the right continued without major changes. Of the five items tested here, women lean to the right on three of the issues: namely, the ban on pornography, legalized school prayers, and recognition of homosexual rights. They reject the restriction of legalized abortion and are divided on the issue of legalized gambling.

TABLE 3.14. CONSERVATISM INDEX

			NI	VP	VA	T&$P	T&$D
1.	Ban on legalized abortion						
	1988	(Female)	8.6	31.9	46.6	8.6	4.3
		(Male)	11.0	27.4	44.5	11.6	5.5
	1989	(Female)	5.4	30.5	48.8	6.9	8.4
		(Male)	5.3	30.3	47.7	9.1	7.6
2.	Ban on legalized gambling						
	1988	(Female)	20.7	35.4	38.4	3.7	1.8
		(Male)	17.7	39.5	36.7	4.8	1.4
	1989	(Female)	13.8	22.2	60.6	.5	3.0
		(Male)	8.2	30.3	56.6	1.9	3.0
3.	Establish antiporn law						
	1988	(Female)	8.8	62.3	20.1	6.3	2.5
		(Male)	8.8	53.1	21.1	12.9	4.1
	1989	(Female)	6.8	73.7	11.2	8.3	
		(Male)	6.5	64.3	22.4	5.3	1.5
4.	Establish school prayer						
	1988	(Female)	19.9	52.8	19.9	6.8	0.6
		(Male)	12.9	59.2	17.0	8.8	2.0
	1989	(Female)	9.8	63.7	22.5	2.9	1.0
		(Male)	9.1	59.1	23.5	5.3	3.0
5.	Establish homosexual rights						
	1988	(Female)	27.8	15.4	48.8	1.2	6.8
		(Male)	23.1	9.5	47.6	.7	19.0
	1989	(Female)	18.6	18.6	58.8	1.0	2.9
		(Male)	14.3	8.7	69.1	.8	7.2

Key: NI = Not Interested, T&$P = Devote Time and Money to Pass,
        VP = Vote to Pass, T&$D = Devote Time and Money to Defeat,
        VA = Vote Against.

Gender Gap

Gender gap first appeared in sociological discourse around the early 1980s. It revolves around different prioritization of electoral issues by the sexes. This survey provides an opportunity to explore gender differentiation with regard to the NCR's ideal of the "proper" role and place for women. A series of chi-square correlations tested the relationship between gender and the attitude indexes. Results are presented in table 3.15.

Looking at correlations for items one to nine (function and place indexes), two conclusions can be drawn: (1) Gender does not reveal a significant relationship with items measuring clear functional duality (items one to three) or female domesticity (items six and seven); (2) Significant correlations between gender and items four, eight, and nine suggest that men are more likely to see a connection between women's nurturing capacity (item four, best occupation for women teaching) and her public or private (item eight, high unemployment, women stay home) roles. Consequently, women's labor market participation is temporary, to be relinquished at times of high unemployment ($x^2=7.54$ for item eight, table 3.15). The phrase, "second income," which often referred to women's earning, reinforces this idea. Similarly, gender affects attitudes toward female socialization. A significant relationship between gender and item nine (girls' education suitable for roles of motherhood and housewife) suggests that men are more likely to support a gender-based education for women.

Jessie Bernard suggests that males and females are born into different worlds in one society (1981). In table 3.15, a correlation of 22.48 between gender and item five attests to this point. Do women have an easier life than men? Sixty-seven percent of women compared to 43 percent of men responded: Definitely Not.

The strongest correlations are observed between gender and attitudes toward the sexes' power in the family and society. Whether at the abstract cognitive level or the practical family level, sex influences respondents' attitude toward power distribution. Men believe that they are better decision makers and that fathers should make important decisions about the future of children (items ten and twelve); meanwhile, they reveal a sense of powerlessness in the family because women hold the real power at home (item twelve, table 3.15). Woman's primordial weakness, as explicated in the Bible, finds more men believers than women supporters (items thirteen and fourteen).

With respect to feminism, significant relationships are observed between gender and items fifteen, sixteen, and nineteen. For item fifteen, 37 percent of men versus 49 percent of women agree that a woman can do anything that a man can. Familial equality measured by item sixteen also receives stronger endorsement from women than men. Gender also affects mistrust of women.

TABLE 3.15. GENDER GAP

	Chi-Square	Significant Level
Function Index		
1	2.14	.5
2	4.44	.2
3	6.63	.08
4	11.09	.01
5	22.48	.000
Place Index		
6	2.42	.84
7	1.30	.72
8	7.54	.05
9	9.31	.02
Power Index		
10	16.09	.001
11	9.88	.01
12	11.29	.01
13	10.24	.01
14	9.45	.02
Feminism Index		
15	8.31	.03
16	9.64	.02
17	4.55	.2
18	4.10	.2
19	8.44	.03

Taken together, the statistical relationships, presented in table 3.15, suggest that both sexes reject extreme spatial and functional segregation. The idea that women's "feminine nature" should dictate their social functions finds more male supporters than female supporters. Therefore, male respondents support some aspects of spatial and functional sex segregation and are more likely to agree with a male-controlled family structure and to believe in women's innate intellectual inferiority.

Conclusion

The rise of religious fundamentalism since the late 1970s has developed into a lingering international trend. In Algeria, Islamic fundamentalists claimed victory in municipal elections forcing the socialist government into making concessions. In America, the conservatives are successfully pushing antiabortion legislature in state assemblies, and just recently the Supreme Court ruled that a ban on nude dancing is constitutional.[6] Family and country are exalted, discrediting liberalism and feminism as branding titles. While the sexual controversies of some television evangelists has dimmed the presence of the New Christian Right in the media, conservatism has become institutionalized.

The NCR has set forth a national agenda to redefine American social, political, and economic priorities. Western Christianity constitutes the interpretive scheme of this restructuring. Gender, family, and the position of women are pivotal themes in this process. The New Christian Right, particularly, is focused to reaffirm traditional sex roles, female domesticity, and feminine occupations for women. The ideal goal is, of course, a utopian, male-centered, female-sustained nuclear "Christian" family. Feminism, gender equality, and power sharing are construed as the enemies of such a family. The same holds true for any program or idea that can remotely be interpreted as against the home-based housewife, such as the Family Leave Act, gun control, and disarmament (Beck, 1992).

But do the majority of American women concur with this new "traditional" course. Does the rise of religious fundamentalism contribute to a new "traditional" identity among women, as well as men?

This study finds that women's response is generally: NO. Women's definition of themselves and their universe is not determined, but connected to, their place in the nuclear family. They disclaim gender as the defining—i.e., limiting—variable of their societal and familial functions and place. It is immature to suggest that American women conceive of their individual identity divorced from its historical foundation, namely the family. In other words, while the American woman rejects a social identity solely construed on the basis of gender and family, family nonetheless remains a major part of her universe of discourse. It seems that the American woman declares, "I am part of the family as it is part of me, but dare not to make it the pivotal point of my existence."

In sum, this survey reveals a rejection of gender based functional and spatial segregation, unidirectional power distribution in the family and the society, and absolute equality of the sexes. Family figures importantly in women's occupational considerations. Women are faced with an "either/or" proposition to choose between family and occupation that is not yet resolved. Feminism, as it is defined here, receives mild support, and women display some degree of group solidarity.

What do American women in this study say about the juxtaposition of modernism and fundamentalism? Female NCR leaders are on record favoring a dualistic vision of fundamentalism: weak in the public domain and strong in the private domain. Patriotism, capitalism, and anticommunism are all core "isms" in the public domain that are favored by the NCR. The female leaders exalt the modernism of the latest weaponry and aggressive patriotism but denounce aggressive feminism in the private domain. As Abbott and Wallace point out, the NCR views "moral authoritarianism" as essential for "unfettered free market capitalism" (1992:101).

The pro-family voice cherishes the complementary gender roles at the family level: a breadwinner husband and a homemaker wife, with the man as the decision maker and feminism as the enemy. Modern ideas of gender equality, shared power, and democratic participation are not welcomed in the domestic domain.

This study shows that the hierarchical sex-role structure advocated by the New Christian Right is not adopted by the majority of women in this sample. However, on several issues, a large minority of about one-third voiced support for some aspects of traditional sex roles advocated by the NCR. For instance, 34 percent of women believe that men are better decision makers than women (item ten, table 3.9); 34 percent see other women as their worst enemies (item, eighteen, table 3.12); 31.7 percent agree that financial independence is detrimental to a woman's happiness (item six, table 3.6); and 36 percent believe that proud husbands dislike for their wives to work (item seven, table 3.6), etc. On social conservatism issues, 32 percent would vote to ban legalized abortion, while over half support prayer in school. One can propose that this is perhaps the core of the New Christian Right's support among women. This approximately 30 percent of women provides a large army of supporters to march, write, contribute, and fight for a Protestantism that is capitalistic, patriotic, and patriarchal.

NOTES

  1. Speer, 1984, provides an illuminating historical background of the New Christian Right. See also Chandler, 1984.

  2. When Schlafly's forty-year-old homosexual son, who lives with his parents, was "outed," she rejected negative labels such as "hypocrite" and called herself "the most tolerant person in the world" (*Newsweek*, 1992:18).

  3. For many men, abortion is the killing of their sperm, which is to them the source of life. Norman Mailer states this the best: "I hate contraception. . . . There is nothing I abhor more than planned parenthood. Planned parenthood is an abomination. If you are not ready to make a baby with that marvelous sex . . . the most marvelous thing that was in you may have been shot into a diaphragm or wasted on a pill" (quoted by Dworkin, 1982:142).

  4. Others have discussed social and individualistic feminism (see Freeman, 1975; Chafe, 1977; Adams and Winston, 1980).

  5. In this, however, they are not consistent and are more responsive to the needs of their business donors and political partners.

For instance, they opposed the Family Leave Act, which would allow a person unpaid leave for the birth or adoption of a child (Beck, 1992).

6. On June 19, 1991, the Louisiana state assembly passed a law banning abortion, to be allowable only in cases of rape, incest, and mother's health under specific conditions. On June 21, 1991, the Supreme Court declared that a ban on nude dancing is constitutional.

CHAPTER FOUR

Egyptian Women's Response to Discourse on Fundamentalism

Introduction

The postwar period witnessed a Westernization trend in many Middle Eastern countries as a consequence of which some aspects of women's roles, particularly in urban areas, changed. Increased participation of women in educational and occupational activities, delayed marriage, legal changes in *Shariat*, and decreased use of the veil gave the impression of declining significance of spatial duality in favor of functional duality.

When, in the late 1970s, young college students in major urban centers of the region started wearing Islamic *hijab* and criticized Western values and life-style, observers dismissed them as rebellious youth rejecting parental authority. Today, women's status is central to the fundamentalists' claim to legitimacy. Women, as supporters and opponents of the movement, are engaged in redrawing spatial boundaries and with it redefining their societal identity. Caught between rapid technological changes, all Western, and their desire to Islamicize the whole social structure, the Islamic fundamentalists, like their fellow believers in other faiths, have opted for a split fundamentalism: modern in the public domain and traditional in the private.

About a half century after Huda Sharawi discarded her veil as a symbol of servitude, young Egyptian women started wearing Islamic *hijab* as a symbol of pride and independence. What seemed in the beginning to be a fad or the youth's rebellion has grown into a full-blown movement. To many observers, it seems that women's emancipation in Egypt has come full circle. To understand this seemingly sudden change, it is necessary to review, in brief, the history of feminism in Egypt.

History of Feminism in Egypt

The Egyptian feminist movement started in the last decade of the nineteenth century. At that time, Egypt was under the colonial domination of Britain.

The debate about the feminist movement in Egypt overflows with discourse on colonization and Westernization. This debate is still as timely and contentious as ever. Were feminists' concerns authentic and indigenous? Were the early women's advocates in Egypt, particularly men, inspired by a genuine desire to liberate Egyptian women? Did they draw their inspiration from their native culture, or was Egyptian feminism a by-product of colonizers' ideology and motivated by class interest of its advocates? Here again, the issue of gender overlaps with nationalism, colonialism, class, and even ethnic boundaries.

A book by Qassim Amin entitled *Women's Emancipation,* published in 1899, formulated the main issues of the discourse on women's rights. In this book, he pointed out the contradiction between the scripture and practice regarding women's treatment. He raised questions about the seclusion of middle-class women, extreme unilateral male rights, and prevalent degrading attitudes toward women as subhumans. In retrospect, his views and those of his opponents were shaped by the discourse of colonialization, Western influence, and the juxtaposition of Islam and Christianity. For some, he is the indisputable father of the feminist movement in Egypt. Abdel Kader sees him as "visionary" and commends him for putting the issue of women's emancipation on the "agenda of public debate" (1987:61). She further refers to his "piercing analysis of prevailing morality" (ibid.:60).

According to Abdel Kader, some of those who criticized Amin were motivated by nationalism, but then there was "opposition from every conservative quarter: The Khadive, the Muslim conservatives and the extreme nationalists" (ibid.:58).

The nationalists raised two major objections: First, they claimed that raising the issue of women, when national independence was at stake, was divisive and unnecessary. Second, "the violence of reaction was rather an expression of aversion to the idea of the Westernization implicit and sometimes explicit in Amin's approaches and themes" (ibid.:61). For many, admitting that colonizers might be right about some aspects of the local culture is tantamount to treason. This debate is still timely and current in the Middle East.

Ahmed, on the other hand, poses the issue from a different perspective. According to her, Amin's motivation was not inherently feminist. Rather, his feminism was Western and shaped by the colonialists' ideology. Ahmed suggests that "as Europeans established themselves as colonial powers in Muslim countries" (1992:150), their racist discourse of exploitation and domination made woman and her status the centerpiece of their ideology. Europe's new colonial discourse claimed that "Islam was innately and immutably oppressive toward women, that the veil and segregation epitomized that oppression, and that these customs were the fundamental reasons for the general and comprehensive backwardness of Islamic societies" (ibid.:151–2). Ahmed suggests that Amin and other feminists from the upper class who benefited from the British domination were emulating the Western colonizers' discourse rather than addressing Egyptian women's concern. "The idea to which Comer and missionaries gave expression formed the basis of Amin's book" (ibid.:155). To Ahmed, Amin's admiration for Western technology and culture made his feminism insincere.

Phillip (1978) propounds the same idea about social background and political orientation of the early feminists. He reports that women feminists focused on the concerns of middle- and upper-class women, and that their activism lacked any nationalism and patriotic expression. Badran replies that "women's feminism in Egypt has been indigenous" (1989:156). Women of all ranks motivated by their own socioeconomic and psychological needs were mobilized to address women's concern within Islamic and nationalist frameworks. Although some issues were concerns of the upper and middle classes, such as seclusion, the basic restrictions on all women remained central. Thus, "Egyptian feminism transcends class" (ibid.:156).

There is a dialectical relationship between women's and nationalist movements. Women's emancipation without national independence is meaningless and empty, while national independence does not guarantee women's rights (see also Jayawardena, 1986). Indeed, after independence women are often told that their services are no longer required and they can return to their "proper" place. Nationalists, whether left or right, regard women's rights as secondary to any nationalist agenda. Any call for women's (or, for that matter, racial or ethnic) rights is perceived as antinationalistic and divisive, a ploy of outside agitators. For instance, after the victory of the Islamic revolution, the Ayatollah Khomeini decreed veiling mandatory for all women. A large number of women in the capital and some other cities showed their opposition in street demonstrations and letter writing. The leftists and radical organizations boycotted these demonstrations and planned alternative demonstrations to distract attention from this group. This author was present in many debates in which the leftists ridiculed the women and branded their concerns as trivial and their intention as a division in the ranks of nationalist forces against foreign imperialism.

In Egypt, the nationalists of left and right opposed Amin's call for the emancipation of women with the same fervor. They perceived the issue of women's emancipation with suspicion as a ploy of Western powers to corrupt the society, undermine the family, and usurp Islamic principles. A leading opponent of women's emancipation was the leader of the Al-Hizb al-Watani who "viewed the emancipation of women in particular as an unpatriotic development that aimed to undermine Egyptian national identity" (Abdel Kadar, 1987:62). Ethnic groups that demand their political rights face the same suspicion and derision. Not surprisingly, many Americans, including some politicians, perceived the civil rights movement as a ploy of the Communists. The issue of women's rights, additionally, attacks every man's individual honor and his proprietary pride and is invariably more sensitive. An opponent of Amin, Talbot Harb, in several publications, accused Amin and those who advocated women's rights as being supported by the British in order to split the nationalist camp and disgrace Islamic women (Sullivan, 1986).

Among others who championed the cause of women's rights was Muhammad Abdu, Amin's teacher. Writing in the 1880s, he warned Muslim societies to reevaluate their antiquated practices and to revive their true Islamic culture in order to stop foreign domination (Esposito, 1982). Among these practices, family, marriage, and treatment of women should be changed to fit the true Islamic teachings (Ahmed, 1992). Badran and others have chronicled the efforts of women feminists such as Aisha Taimuriyya (1840–1902), who wrote poetry and stories describing her resentment against seclusion. Nabawiyya Musa was the first woman to take the secondary school exam, despite British objections, and obtain a certificate (Ahmed, 1992:171). Despite strong opposition, Amin's works, coupled with other historical events of the time, inspired other men and women who were sympathetic to the women's cause. Malak Hifni Nasif (1886–1918) was one of this group. Due to her upbringing, and later inspired by Amin's works, she spoke against polygamy, early marriage, unilateral divorce, etc. Well grounded in *Quranic* teachings, she was more careful not to praise Western ideals and behaviors.

Generally, the feminist discourse revolved around variations of "relational feminism," as suggested by Offen (1988). The woman's social existence was seen based on her place in the family, "not as a human individual" (Phillip, 1978:286). The feminists framed their debate within the framework of national independence and economic autonomy, explicitly or implicitly. They reiterated that to regenerate the society, the family must be reformed and that this could only be achieved if women's fate is improved. Women need to be educated to raise worthy citizens. This entails realistic and concrete goals of education, family security, and financial protection. Today, Islamic feminists forward a similar notion of women's rights (see Hoffman-Ladd, 1987).

As far as the sociopolitical and economic structures of the country were concerned, Muhammad Ali, a governor appointed by the Ottomans and later the British, established a state bureaucracy, reformed state finances, improved agricultural production, and reorganized the military. At the outbreak of

World War I, Egypt was officially a British protectorate. The war temporarily quelled the nationalist movement. After the war, the nationalists, under the leadership of Saad Zaghlul, were organized into the Wafd party. One of the leaders of the party was Ali Sharawi, Huda Sharawi's husband.

Huda Sharawi, born into the Egyptian nobility, after a life of seclusion in a harem and an early marriage, became the acknowledged leader of Egyptian feminism. She also played an active role in the nationalist movement. Indeed, when several leaders of the Wafd party were sent into exile, she organized harem women in opposition to the British domination and led them in street demonstrations (March 1919). Later, she organized the first political organization of women as part of the Wafd party. Like many other women's organizations at a time of national crisis, this organization played an important role in the nationalist movement. However, after independence (February 1922) women were not allowed to share in the rewards. They were not even allowed in the opening ceremony of the first parliament, and the constitution did not recognize their right to political participation. As Badran indicates, "The promises, implicit and explicit, the Wafd had made to the women in the course of their national struggle to draw them into the life of the nation once independence was achieved, were conveniently forgotten by the men" (quoted by Abdel Kader, 1987:153.)

Disappointed, Sharawi and her associates formed the Egyptian Feminist Union (March 1923) to participate in the Ninth Congress of the International Women's Suffrage Alliance in Rome. It was in returning from this meeting that Sharawi and her group, in a dramatic gesture, removed their veils in public. The Egyptian Feminist Union campaigned on behalf of women's social and human rights and achieved some of its goals, such as public education for girls and women's entry into universities. But their substantive demands for reform of family laws and women's suffrage were ignored and rejected. Later, similar organizations, like the Daughters of the Nile, were created to campaign for the same goals.

Parallel with political and social organizations, women's groups engaged in social and philanthropic activities by providing educational, health and child care, and similar services for women. Abdel Kadar estimates that there were about 156 women's organizations in the 1950s (1987:99). By working in public, these women "made social work respectable. By extension and time, all work, paid or unpaid, became respectable" (ibid.). Nevertheless, women's gains from the 1930s until the mid-1950s remained minimal. The death of Huda Sharawi in 1947 deprived the movement of its brave and innovative leader.

Until the takeover of the state by the Free Officers (July 1952), women activists were mostly engaged in social services programs. The socialist leaders launched a program to reform the social, economic, and political structures of Egypt. Nasser's government made education a high priority, with emphasis on compulsory education for both boys and girls and a literacy campaign. Reorganization of the economy, reform of labor laws, and increased day care facilities provided more employment opportunities for women in the formal sector. In the political scene, women were given the vote and managed to elect a few women to political offices. With regard to family issues, the area that received the highest attention was family planning and health care for women and children.

The socialist era (1952–74) almost ended with the sudden death of President Nasser but was formally closed by the declaration of the October Papers by President Saddat. The open-door policy, known as *Infitah*, reversed state planning in favor of a laissez-faire economy, foreign investment, private production, and relaxed government regulations.

The period that started in 1979 and lasted until 1985 witnessed several contradictory changes in women's legal status. In 1979, the peace treaty between Egypt and Israel was signed. The parliament was then dissolved and a new election held. The constitution was revised, including provisions for women's rights. The People's Assembly (*Majlis al Shaab*) was enlarged to accommodate thirty reserved seats for women, and women were guaranteed seats in local councils. During the absence of the parliament, a presidential decree amended the Personal Status Law, which was later ratified by the new parliament. Mrs. Saddat was instrumental in issuance of this decree, which was often referred to as "Jihan's Laws" (Sullivan, 1986:37).

This decree instituted a series of restrictions on a man's right to polygamous marriage, child custody, and divorce. Women became entitled to alimony and gained child custody rights, were allowed to remain in the matrimonial home while having custody of children, etc. Later the constitutionality of this law was questioned, and finally in 1985 it was invalidated by the Higher Constitutional Court. Later the same year, a watered-down version of the 1979 law was passed (ibid.:37).

The socioeconomic changes of the *Infitah* affected women's position in the labor market and the family. As with similar policies elsewhere (for instance, Brazil and Iran.), the Saddat-Mubarak open-door policy brought economic growth without economic development (Amin, 1981), which is said to be partly responsible for the rise of Islamic fundamentalism in Egypt. A partnership between national and foreign capital has increased investment and improved job opportunities for both men and women. A shift in the economy from agriculture to capital-intensive industry and services has induced rural to urban migration (Moghadam, 1993). The major beneficiaries of these changes are the urban upper and middle classes. Despite the economic growth, the gap between rich and poor has widened. Reduced government services and removal of subsidies from daily essentials, coupled with inflation, has brought hardship for those who have not benefited from the economic boom.

In addition to economic disparity, cultural changes have alienated a large segment of the population. Western technology and capital bring an aspect of Western culture to the less developed countries that is superficial, consumer oriented, and secular. This cultural invasion promotes xenophobia among many urban strata. This is what Al Ahmad (1977) has called "Westoxication." This veneer of Westernization/modernization appeals to the new bourgeoisie and the middle class who can afford the new Western status symbols. But it alienates the traditional bourgeoisie, particularly workers and peasants who have lost in the process of economic transformation. This is where the battle between modernism and fundamentalism intensifies.

The failure of Western developmental approaches, accompanied by the Palestinian issue and various miniwars with the West (Dophar, the Gulf), have left a deep sense of inferiority and frustration in the Middle Eastern psyche. The new Islamic nationalism spreading throughout the region is fundamentalist, patriarchal, and anti-West. A combination of these and other regional factors (like the Islamic Revolution in Iran) has accelerated a return to traditional values. In the case of Egypt, the Islamic dogma was never removed from the everyday life of citizens. Secularization is superficial. A majority of the country rely on Islamic principles and Arabic heritage for a normative order and their self-identity.

Considering the discord caused by the colonial denigration of local cultures—particularly through treatment of women—Islamic nationalism invariably and inevitably is concerned with women and the protection of the private domain. Marshall suggests that "Muslim revolutionaries . . . utilized Islam . . . in the fight for political autonomy . . . [and] to mount a holy war against the infidels. This intertwined . . . with the defense of the traditional Muslim family, particularly in regions where colonial assimilation policies were directed at women" (1984:5).

Colonizers attacked the family to uproot resistance. In their quest for hegemonic control, the colonizers regarded faith and family as the bastion of indigenous culture and perhaps the breeding ground for resistance. In this regard, missionaries forced conversion and proselytized an antitraditional ethos. Frantz Fanon articulates the general sentiment when he addresses the French anti-veil policies: "Every veil that fell, every body that offered itself to the bold and important glance of the occupier was a negative expression of the fact that Algeria was beginning to deny herself and was accepting the rape of the colonizer" (1965:42).

In the Muslim Middle Eastern countries, colonizers formulated a pseudoscientific theory of Islamic androcentricity. Islam is inherently backward and antiquated. It isolates and denigrates women and treats them as subhuman. To civilize Middle Easterners, Islam should be weakened and Christianity promoted. To this end, women were important players as mothers who mold the next generation and as symbols. Thus, the discarding of the veil became integral to the colonizers' hegemonic policies and later to the modernization policies of the state in Turkey and Iran.

Ahmed poses the interaction of colonialism and feminism in an interesting light. She reveals how the Victorian men who opposed and ridiculed British women's demand for the franchise "captured the language of feminism and redirected it, in the service of colonialism, toward Other men and the cultures of Other men" (1992:151). She discloses that Comer, the governor general of Egypt who championed the unveiling of Egyptian women, was founder of the "Men's League for Opposing Women's Suffrage" in England (ibid.: 153).

Najmabadi relates an editorial from a woman's magazine in Iran that echoes the same idea: "Woman is the best means of destroying indigenous culture to the benefit of Imperialists" (1991:67). The singular theme of these ideas stated by a secular feminist and an Islamic feminist denotes the intensity and depth of this cultural discord in Middle Eastern consciousness. Feminists and fundamentalists agree on the exploitation of women by the colonizers and the imperialists.

One should not, however, overlook the effect of industrialization, urbanization, and cultural modernism on these societies. The discourse of veil was not effected by the colonizers alone, but also by Islamic reformers who were genuinely concerned with the antiquated practices of their societies and the stagnant status of Islamic ideology. Modernist thinkers such as Afgani, Muhamad Abdu, and others throughout the region had started a chorus of revitalization and *Ijtihad* (reinterpretation) of Islam (Keddie, 1972, 1983). Woman's status was the recurring theme in this dialogue. Many had realized that the structural changes were impossible to halt; the moral fabric needed to be reformed to shape and control the effects of the changes.

The nineteenth-century history of Egyptian feminism signals a changing traditional society grappling with modernization and Western penetration. Modernized men and women sought to claim women from the "underlife" of the society (Abdel Kadar, 1987:68). Similarly, Najmabadi suggests that "The traditional woman, for the progressive man of the 19th century became the symbolic location of social backwardness" (1991:70). To this end, the veil, the most poignant symbol of traditionalism, must be removed with fanfare, as in Egypt, Turkey, and Iran.

From a parade of colonizers, modernists, and now fundamentalists, woman's body and her symbolic presentation served to signal a changing trend. With each trend, a new configuration of faith, family, and state reshaped the public and private status of women. For the colonizers, the veil and seclusion legitimated the cultural transformation of Muslim colonies. For modernist men, they were embarrassing reminders of traditional culture. This is the group more criticized as the "handmaiden of colonizers" (Ahmed, 1992) or Westoxicated (Gharbzadeh) (Al Ahmad, 1977).

Religious fundamentalism often resonates with some form of symbolism, too. The issue of modesty for Islamic fundamentalists and reproductive rights for Protestant fundamentalists are cases in point. Such a symbolism is appropriately valid for all three domains of faith, family, and state. It connects all three together nicely and reflects the demarcation of the two spheres of public and private. The Islamic *hijab* symbolizes a new cultural discourse: Islamic fundamentalism. At first, it was a novelty, a cause for glances, ridicule, fury, and snickers. I remember vividly how the sign of scarfed women in the courtyard of the law school at the University of Tehran amazed and intrigued me in the mid-1970s. Only a few years earlier, we were clad in awkward miniskirts. Now the next cohort were ignoring a German fashion magazine's (the *Burda*) dictate of public appearance.

Islamic *hijab* is often translated as "veil," which can be misleading since they constitute different meanings and behavioral standards and have distinct social implications. (El Guindi, 1981, and Williams, 1979, make the same point, but use the word veil, nonetheless.) Veil or *hijab* implies a sense of spatial and functional seclusion, which the Islamic *hijab* does not. In this book, I will use the phrase Islamic *hijab*, which is *hijab* Islami in Iran, *al-Ziyy al-Islami* (the Islamic dress) in Egypt, and *burga* in Pakistan.

While there is agreement that this trend goes far beyond symbolism and has far-reaching consequences, there is little consensus about its effects on women's rights. Two narratives have developed in this discourse (Badran, 1994). The one I will call secular feminism responded to the rise of fundamentalism with alarm. Fearing the loss of minor hard-earned human and civil rights the total institutionalization of *Shariat* with its concomitant restrictions on women, many cried for protection of women against the fundamentalists. The appearance of widespread Islamic *hijab*, either mandatory, as in Iran, or strongly urged, as in Egypt, public persecution of women, imposed seclusion, and private abuse of women were major concerns. Indeed, many, including myself, feared the total dehumanization and objectification of women (see Gerami, 1989). Abdel Kader refers to this movement as "retraditionalization of women's status and roles and women's return to their 'proper' place" (1987:137).

Women's pioneering role in the fundamentalist movements and their rejection of western values have given rise to the proposition that there is another brand of feminism in Muslim countries that is conceptually different from Western secular feminism. While the exact components of this ideology are not yet formulated, at least two ideas are clear: In the political scene, women have the right to express their opinions within the framework of Islamic principles; in the family and in the society, sex roles are complementary rather than conflicting and competing. An increased number of women in higher education and in the labor market suggests women's support for equality of employment and educational opportunities. Therefore, it seems that there are elements of secular feminism combined with the Islamic sex-role ascription as part of this Islamic feminism.

El Guindi calls women's return to *hijab* liberating and states, "And so it is in the name of Islam and guided by Muslim ethics that this new Egyptian woman is liberating herself, and her male kin, by choosing to 'veil' and not to be molested or stopped when invading public space with full force, as she is" (1981:483). This narrative is hailed as indigenous, with women taking the initiative to reclaim their bodies from the onslaught of consumerism and capitalism. Its advocates, who do not call themselves feminist, claim that their approach to women's rights will deliver them from exploitation by the colonizers and imperialists. It draws its aspiration from Islam and native culture.

The interaction between the two forms of feminism has a striking resemblance to the interaction of feminists and antifeminists in the United States. Badran expands the dialogue by postulating a three-way interaction between Islamists, feminists, and gender activists in Egypt. The first two groups either publicly pronounce their orientation or engage in activism on related causes. Gender activists are "many women across a broad spectrum [who] insist on maintaining or increasing their own roles in society or promoting a public presence in general" (1994:204).

Today the two narratives of Islamic and secular feminism are more mature and more aware of each other. Women fundamentalists listen and respond to secular feminists and demand their rights in the name of Islam. Meanwhile, we have realized that not all of our fears were well founded. Perhaps we failed to see the resilience and tenacity of Muslim women. Middle and lower middle class women seek education and fiercely compete in matriculation exams for limited seats at the universities. They are particularly interested in the male specialties of medicine and engineering. They work and, despite fundamentalist preaching, remain in the job market after having children. They write and publish more than ever. For the first time, a large number of women are attending women's seminaries, reading and interpreting religious sources. In the long run, this may lead to a feminist interpretation and critique of the *Quran* similar to that already accomplished by Christian and Jewish women with regard to their respective scriptures.

In legal terms, women, whether in Egypt, Iran, or Pakistan, are losing ground in terms of family protection, political rights, and perhaps even employment and educational opportunities. A return to *Shariat* in many countries has eroded a few restrictions on men's unilateral right to divorce, polygamy, child custody, and early marriage. Although women are not banned from higher education, in some countries, like Iran during the first decade after the revolution, they were excluded from "masculine" areas, like engineering, and were encouraged to major in "feminine" disciplines. The oil glut and general depression in the region have eliminated many jobs of guest workers in Arab countries and has reduced the local job market as well. So, repatriated and local workers facing unemployment are calling for women to return to the home and open up jobs for men. Protective laws in Egypt, Iran, and Pakistan are considered or passed to give employed women full and early retirement, mandatory part-time jobs, or to penalize men with working wives through promotion, pay insurance, bonuses, and other measures. Reports on women's participation in the labor market are conflicting. While the percentage of women in the nonagricultural sector has shown a modest increase (World Bank, 1988), there are conflicting reports about their share in the informal and agricultural sectors (see Moghadam, 1993). It is too early to decree the final verdict on the consequences of this movement for women of the region.

What Do Egyptian Women Think?

This study addresses four specific topics: women's role, women's place, women and power, and feminist consciousness. Thus, answers to four questions are explored:

1. Do Egyptian women perceive a functional duality of sex roles?

    (The extent of overlap between these roles)

2. Do Egyptian women see a spatial segregation of the sexes?

    (The extent of their support for sex segregation)

3. How do Egyptian women see their relation to power?

    (The extent of women's power in the family and society)

4. What are Egyptian women's response to feminism?

    (The extent of their support for sexual equality)

Research Design

To measure women's perception of place versus functional duality, a questionnaire was developed. Two scales dealt specifically with women's place versus her role. Another scale measured women's perception of power and their handling of power. One scale measured group consciousness and the extent of support for feminist issues.

Previous studies have clearly indicated that Islamic fundamentalism is a middle-class phenomenon (Mernissi, 1987). All members of this sample were middle-class women from Cairo. A survey questionnaire was administered to a sample of 120 women in Cairo in 1989. Eighty-eight completed questionnaires were returned. Later, in 1991, another sample from a different neighborhood in Cairo was tested. This time seventy-five questionnaires were returned. This sample provided the same result. The main difference was in their educational and occupational backgrounds. A larger percentage of this group had college degrees and more were employed. Nevertheless, their attitudes toward the issues were not different from the original sample.

TABLE 4.1. GENERAL CHARACTERISTICS OF THE EGYPTIAN SAMPLE (%)

Employment		Yrs Employed		Education		Marital		# Children		Age	
Ft	20.5	1-5	27.3	< Hs	1.1	M	72.2	1-2	15.9	> 20	4.5
Pt	28.4	6-10	12.5	Hs	17.0	S	22.7	3-4	51.1	21-30	53.4
Hsw	24.0	11-15	4.5	2 Cl	15.9	W	1.1	5-7	13.6	31-40	33.0
Ret	10.2	16-20	6.8	Cl	40.0	D	2.3	> 7	2.3	41-50	6.5
Std	15.9	>20	5.7	> Cl	25.0	N/A	17.0	N/A	34.1	> 50	4.8

Key: Ft = Full Time , Pt = Part Time, Hsw = Housewife, Ret = Retired,
Std = Student, Hs = High School, Cl = College, M=Married, S=Single,
W=Widowed, D=Divorced, N/A = Not Applicable
This table does not include missing cases.

Background Information

Table 4.1 shows some background information on the respondents. As the table indicates, this group was among the highly educated (40 percent had a college degree), young (the majority under the age of 40), and married with children. Almost equal numbers were employed and housewives. Among the employed, professional occupations like physicians, college professors, and accountants, as well as white-collar workers like secretaries, sales persons, and beauticians were represented. About 16 percent were students.

Feminine/Masculine Functions

A scale with five items measured attitudes toward woman's proper role. Table 4.2 presents an English translation of the items with descriptive statistics for the scale. As the means and standard deviations show, there is some consistency among respondents with regard to woman's proper place. Three questions in particular, dealing with the primacy of man's occupation and the wife's responsibility to support his job (items one, two, and four), show that women agree on the greater importance of a man's job compared to a woman's job. It seems that women agree that their primary function is motherhood. Agreeing on their primary function, they then disagree on their other options. Questions three and five, dealing with woman's role only as a mother and housewife or only in feminine occupations, such as teaching, received mixed responses. Looking at the descriptive statistics and frequency distributions for these items, it is clear that women are divided on this issue. While they agree that their primary function is motherhood, they disagree if it should be their only function.

TABLE 4.2. WOMEN'S FUNCTION INDEX

		Mean	Median	Stdev
1.	Men's happiness is social position	1.87	2.0	1.00
2.	Woman give up her job interfere family	1.42	1.0	.83
3.	Men's job is to bring money, women's is family	2.64	3.0	1.14
4.	Woman emphasizes husband's job, more than hers	1.49	1.0	.74
5.	Best occupation for women is teaching	2.37	2.0	1.06

TABLE 4.3. WOMEN'S FUNCTION: % DISTRIBUTION

		SA	AS	DS	SD
1.	Men's happiness is social position	48.3	26.4	15.0	10.0
2.	Woman give up her job interfere family	73.3	18.6	1.20	7.0
3.	Men's job is to bring money, women's is family	19.5	30.0	17.2	33.3
4.	Woman emphasizes husband's job, more than hers	63.1	27.4	7.1	2.4
5.	Best occupation for women is teaching	24.7	33.0	23.5	18.8

Key: SA = Strongly Agree, AS = Agree Somewhat, DS = Disagree Somewhat, SD= Strongly Disagree.

Table 4.4 shows a correlation matrix between the items of this scale. Of interest is the strong bivariate relationship between items three and five (*r*=.34), providing further support for the above points.[1]

Private/Public Spheres

Another scale with six questions was designed to measure women's attitudes toward spatial segregation of the sexes. As the means and standard deviation in table 4.5 show, two trends are again observable. Means (2.57 and 3.33) and standard deviations (.79 and .97) for items seven and eleven show that women do not support being secluded. Frequency distributions in table 4.6 show that about 70 percent of respondents clearly reject the notion that a woman's place is in the private domain.

TABLE 4.4. WOMEN'S FUNCTION: CORRELATION MATRIX

	1	2	3	4	5
1		.24*	.05	.11	.1
2			.40*	.23*	.26*
3				.06	.34*
4					.44*
5					

* *P* = <.05.

TABLE 4.5. WOMEN'S PLACE INDEX

		Mean	Median	Stdev
6.	Women's happiness is homemaking, regardless of her achievement outside	2.43	2.5	1.18
7.	Want outside job not natural (less feminine)	2.57	4.0	.79
8.	Proud husband dislikes wife to work	2.89	3.0	1.12
9.	High unemployment, women stay home	1.82	1.0	.99
10.	Girl ed suitable roles: mother and housewife	1.98	2.0	1.0
11.	Boys' happiness ed, girls' marriage	3.33	4.0	.97

TABLE 4.6. WOMEN'S PLACE: % DISTRIBUTION

		SA	AS	DS	SD
6.	Women's happiness is homemaking, regardless of her achievement outside	3.2	18.2	25.0	25.0
7.	Want outside job not natural (less feminine)	3.4	8.1	17.0	71.6
8.	Proud husband dislikes wife to work	18.4	12.6	31.0	37.9
9.	High unemployment, women stay home	50.6	26.4	13.8	9.2
10.	Girl ed suitable roles: mother and housewife	40.2	33.3	14.9	11.5
11.	Boys happiness ed, girls' marriage	8.0	11.5	19.5	60.9

Key: SA = Strongly Agree, AS = Agree Somewhat, DS = Disagree Somewhat, SD = Strongly Disagree.

TABLE 4.7. WOMEN'S PLACE: CORRELATION MATRIX

	6	7	8	9	10	11
6		.12	$.35^*$	$.32^*$	$.37^*$	$.21^*$
7			$.23^*$	-.03	-.06	$.21^*$
8				$.19^*$	$.25^*$	$.19^*$
9					$.37^*$	-.09
10						$.23^*$
11						

* $P = <.05$.

Rejecting restrictions on their place does not weaken their support for their family responsibilities. Women, again, place emphasis on man's job and their role as mother. Questions nine and ten, dealing with woman's duty during unemployment and girl's education suitable for motherhood, with means of 1.82 and 1.98 and standard deviations of .99 and 1.0, respectively, suggest that functional duality is more acceptable than spatial duality to women.

According to the literature and Islamic scripture, men are guardians of women, both spiritually and physically. A man's honor is closely linked to the behavior of his womenfolk. To safeguard their honor, men prefer to seclude women. Question eight directly asks women if proud husbands dislike their wives to work. A mean of 2.89 and the proportion of disagreement over agreement of 2.22 suggest that women believe this not to be true. But a standard deviation of 1.12 also points out that women are not clear about men's preference. A comparable sample of men would have shed some light on this issue.

Question six addresses the same issue in more general terms, stating "a woman's happiness is inside home, regardless of her achievement outside home." Results are very similar to those of question eight with a mean of 2.43 and standard deviation of 1.18. A bivariate correlation between these items (r=.35) in table 4.7 shows that they are closely related. In addition to a statistically significant correlation with item eight, question six is also correlated with items nine (r=.32) and ten (r=.37). Looking at the three tables for this index, it is clear that women support sex-role specialization but they do not support spatial segregation. This scale supports the results of the previous index, which shows that women put emphasis on their nurturing roles as mothers and housewives; it also indicates that they reject seclusion because of these roles. It seems again that women support functional duality more than spatial duality.

Women and Power

Another scale with six items measured women's relation to power. Questions twelve and thirteen seek information about women's general ideas regarding their ability to make decisions and handle power. Means of 2.39 for both and standard deviations of .85 and 1.0, respectively, in table 4.8, show consistency. A standard deviation of .85 for item twelve shows that women are clearly in agreement about their inadequacy in making important decisions. This is consistent with their response to question fifteen, asking about the role of the father in the future plans of children. A combination of these items (twelve, thirteen, and fifteen) shows that women do not see themselves as power holders and decision makers. If we add item fourteen about women's power at home, the picture becomes even more clear. Women believe they are not suitable to hold power and they do not do so.

Since the Islamic movement has led to the politicization of women, it is essential to explore their attitudes toward power and their relation to it at home and in the public domain. Islamic scripture is very specific about the "inherent" inability of women to handle power or to make rational decisions. Causal links are drawn between woman's weaker physical structure and her intellectual inferiority. It is further proposed, and taken as proven fact, that woman's delicate physique and weak mind make her unsuitable for politics and the judiciary.

TABLE 4.8. WOMEN'S RELATION TO POWER INDEX

		Mean	Median	Stdev
12.	Women incapable of making important decisions	2.39	2.0	.85
13.	Men more capable of handling power	2.39	2.0	1.0
14.	Women have power at home	2.75	3.0	1.06
15.	Father important decisions for future children	2.22	2.0	1.06
16.	Weaker psych = weaker mental psych	3.45	4.0	.97
17.	No intellec. strength for judiciary/politics	3.21	4.0	.99

Taken together, these four items suggest that at an abstract level women do not see themselves as power holders and decision makers, and at a concrete level they do not believe they have or should have equal power with men.

TABLE 4.9. RELATION TO POWER: % DISTRIBUTION

	SA	AS	DS	SD
12. Women incapable of making important decisions	11.3	51.1	25.0	12.5
13. Men more capable of handling power	23.9	31.8	26.1	18.2
14. Women have power at home	15.9	23.9	29.5	30.7
15. Father important decisions for future children	31.8	30.7	21.6	15.9
16. Weaker psych = weaker mental psych	9.3	5.8	15.1	69.8
17. No intellec. strength for judiciary/politics	9.3	12.8	25.6	52.3

Key: SA = Strongly Agree, AS = Agree Somewhat, DS = Disagree Somewhat,
        SD= Strongly Disagree.

However, women strongly reject the idea that they are fundamentally incapable of power management. Islamic literature contains references to woman's physical and mental weakness and her emotional instability. For these reasons women are barred from the judiciary and politics. Questions sixteen and seventeen with means of 3.45 and 3.21, respectively, and standard deviations of .97 and .99, resectively, for both, show that women strongly disagree with this Islamic principle.

Altogether, these six items imply three points:

1. Women do not concede that they are innately inadequate to handle power and make rational decisions.

2. They agree in general that they are not competent power holders or decision makers.

3. When it comes to practical matters, they delegate decision making and power to men.

The apparent inconsistency between the first point and the last two is due to the difference between theory and practice. Women reject the notion that they are ill-equipped to hold power, but they realize that men are power holders and make important decisions. This also could be due to socialization. Men are socialized to hold power and are more experienced in making decisions. Women recognize this and prefer to allow them to continue.

Table 4.10 reflects correlations between these items. Strong bivariate correlations between twelve and thirteen ($r=.35$), thirteen and fifteen ($r=.28$), and sixteen and seventeen ($r=.44$) support the previous argument.

TABLE 4.10. RELATION TO POWER: CORRELATION MATRIX

	12	13	14	15	16	17
12		.35[*]	.1	.20[*]	.19[*]	.23[*]
13			-.03	.28[*]	.20[*]	.21[*]
14				.21[*]	.01	.10
15					.16	.14
16						.44[*]
17						

[*] $P = <.05.$

Feminism

A scale with seven items designed to gauge women's attitudes on feminist issues ranging from financial and educational opportunities for women to solidarity and group consciousness provides conflicting results. Tables 4.11 and 4.12 show descriptive statistics and frequency distributions for this category.

TABLE 4.11. FEMINISM INDEX

		Mean	Median	Stdev
18.	Women can perform any job men can	2.22	2.0	1.00
19.	Financial independence detrimental to happiness	3.22	3.5	.91
20.	Educational materials girls = boys	1.70	1.0	.94
21.	Worst enemies of women other women	2.47	2.0	1.17
22.	Cannot trust a woman with a secret	2.59	2.0	1.16
23.	Fair to expect husband to help with chores	2.04	2.0	.93
24.	Easier to talk to women than husband	3.27	4.0	1.07

TABLE 4.12. FEMINISM INDEX: % DISTRIBUTION

		SA	AS	DS	SD
18.	Women can perform any job men can	27.3	36.4	22.7	13.6
19.	Financial independence detrimental to happiness	4.6	19.3	26.1	50.0
20.	Educational materials girls = boys	57.5	20.7	16.1	5.7
21.	Worst enemies of women other women	27.4	27.4	16.7	28.6
22.	Cannot trust a woman with a secret	22.4	28.2	17.6	31.8
23.	Fair to expect husband to help with chores	32.6	39.5	19.8	8.1
24.	Easier to talk to women than husband	11.6	11.6	15.1	61.6

Key: SA = Strongly Agree, AS = Agree Somewhat, DS = Disagree Somewhat,
         SD= Strongly Disagree.

The first item asks a general question about equality between the sexes. A mean of 2.22 and a standard deviation of 1.0, and a 1.8 proportion of agreement over disagreement suggest a moderate support for equality of sexes. Equalitarian relationship in the household responsibilities, measured by item twenty-three, also receives moderate support from the respondents.

Measuring another aspect of gender inequality, items nineteen and twenty deal with financial independence and educational opportunities for women. Question nineteen states "financial independence for women is detrimental to their happiness." A mean of 3.22 and a standard deviation of .91 show that women strongly reject this notion. Respondents' support for equal education for boys and girls is supported by a mean of 1.70 and standard deviation of .94 for item twenty.

Items twenty-one, twenty-three, and twenty-four were designed to gain a measure of group solidarity and cohesiveness among women. As the means, and standard deviations, as well as percentages, show, there is very little sense of group solidarity among the respondents. Indeed, there seems to be a lack of trust for women, which is also supported by the bivariate correlations, in table 4.13, between items twenty-one and twenty-two ($r=.61$) and items twenty-two and twenty-four ($r=.19$). It seems that when it comes to supporting women's access to education and financial independence women can rally around these points, but they do not rely on their sisters to gain these rights.

TABLE 4.13. FEMINISM INDEX: CORRELATION MATRIX

	18	19	20	21	22	23	24
18	.19*	-.03	.11	-.02	-.14	-.04	
19		.14	.08	.12	.12	-.05	
20			.20*	.01	-.10	.10	
21				.61*	.10	.10	
22					-.10	.19*	
23						.00	
24							

* $P = <.05$.

The result of this index provides one piece of concrete information and that is lack of group solidarity among the respondents. Some ethnographic studies have documented the existence of a network of relatives and friends among the women of the Middle East (Friedl, 1989; Altorki, 1986). It is possible that practical everyday reliance on other women is not translated into an ideology of solidarity and group cohesiveness.

As far as feminism is concerned, this scale reveals some support for gender equality. This could be support for expanding opportunities for women rather than acknowledging equality of the sexes. A scale constructed within the framework of the Islamic sex-role provisions might provide a different picture of feminism in Egypt.

Conclusion

This survey explored women's perception of spatial versus functional duality of sex roles. It also examined if these theoretical constructs are supported by women's cognitive recognition or if, at a practical level, they blend to the point of being indistinguishable. The results show that women identify functional duality to be more important than spatial segregation. They clearly identify separate functions for men and women and recognize feminine functions as women's primary responsibilities. Recognizing that, they then reject restrictions on their opportunities in the job market.

With regard to the dichotomies, this research identifies three areas for future research: (a) women's rejection of their spatial seclusion despite their feminine functions; (b) the overlap between the dichotomies; and (c) feminine occupations as women's outlet in the labor market.

The result for women's relation to power and their capacity for rational judgment indicates two points: (a) rejection of women's fundamental inferiority; and (b) their belief in their inadequacy to make important decisions and hold power. While there is some support for their reluctance to assume power (item fifteen), there is strong evidence that they believe men are better decision makers. This suggests women have not internalized the ideology rationalizing patriarchy, but have been socialized to accept it as practical. Two areas call for further clarification: women's power at home and accepted level of sexual equality with regard to power, if any.

Finally, with regard to feminism, clear conceptualization of Islamic and secular feminism is needed. We further need to weigh the role of the former in women's rights in the region.

This research calls into question findings of case studies documenting women's reliance on each other as an indicator of a cognitive level of group solidarity. One must be careful not to interpret women's reliance on each other for child care or other supportive services as indications of trust necessary for group solidarity. Given the traditional hostilities between in-laws and fear of polygamous marriage, it is possible that practical dependence on other women does not eliminate lack of trust and fear of competition. In other words, the traditional relationships of the extended family, which make services and dependence upon each other possible, also prohibit trust and the cameraderie of group cohesiveness. This lack of trust could be a deliberate and conscious result of traditional experience rather than a result of false consciousness.

NOTE

1. A series of factorials were calculated to further explore these findings and to test for underlying patterns of relationships among the items.

CHAPTER FIVE

The Fundamentalist State and Middle-Class Iranian Women

Introduction

The focus of this chapter is urban middle-class women's definition of their role and place in the Islamic Republic of Iran. The rise of Islamic fundamentalism provides a unique opportunity to explore women's attitudes toward their proper role and place. In addition to redefining women's status, Islamic fundamentalism has also affected their power in the family and society: directly, by redefining women's role and place, and indirectly, through their participation in the movement. Increased politicization due to participation in a movement contributes to empowerment. As a result, one can predict that women will express more willingness to hold and exercise power in the family and society. Closely tied to the above factors is an increased sense of group identity and solidarity among women.

A survey analysis of middle-class Iranian women measures their attitudes toward spatial versus functional distinctions of sex roles, their relation to power at home and in society, and their extent of feminist consciousness against the background of the fundamentalist movement.

The Islamic Republic of Iran, constituted in 1980, is the only republic based on Islamic doctrine. Saudi Arabia and Kuwait are traditional nonrepresentative Islamic states. The Islamic Republic of Iran is also the result of an Islamic revolution. Other religious movements in the region, some older, have not been successful in overthrowing semisecular states in Egypt, Algeria, or Pakistan.

From the beginning, the revolution and later the republic, by design or default, had to formulate some form of gender discourse. The state's legitimacy is based on Islamic fundamentalism, managing a two-pronged tactic of resisting imperialist intervention and safeguarding the patriarchal family against modernism. These campaigns are intertwined to the extent that one's contour forms the other's structure.

A fetishized form of female honor symbolizes the state's control of antirevolutionary forces and its strength against foreign interventions. As Jalal states about Pakistan after the independence, "the emphasis on women's security was, in many respects, a sublimation of the broader concerns about security of the state. The analogy is of some value in understanding the difference in relationship between women and state in the colonial and postcolonial periods. So long as the British remained at the helm, political accommodations aimed at circumscribing state intervention in the domestic arena. With the departure of colonial rulers, the state was the ultimate guarantor of the social order whose moral underpinnings were symbolized by women" (1991:85–6).

The Pahlavi regime's legitimacy was not tied to women's status or even the family; rather it demanded allegiance because of its modernization and Westernization of the country and social institutions, including the family. Thus, the de-traditionalization of middle-class women was important in its de-legitimacy. Among the many complaints against the Phalavis, such as the corruption of the royal court, political oppression, and inflation, the women's question found a place of prominence. The Pahlavi regime was one of those modernist states that was embarrassed by the traditional gender structure and tried to modernize and Westernize female symbolism by removing the veil. For the same reason, women demonstrators during the revolution felt obligated—though not forced—to wear *chador* (full-length veil). Although not recognized by most observers at the time, veiled women demonstrators solidified the *hijab* and female modesty as symbols of the new regime.

The early signs of Islamic fundamentalism among women was observable before the revolution. College and high school students started wearing the Islamic *hijab* as a sign of resistance against the Pahlavi regime in the early 1970s. Despite the regime's policy of banning *hijab* in schools and workplaces, *hijab* spread rapidly. During the revolution, *hijab* and *chador* became women's symbol of resistance. Many of those who donned the *hijab* voluntarily as a sign of solidarity with the movement did not intend and could not foresee its becoming a mandatory dress and behavior code. The Ayatollah's decree in early March of 1979 that all working women should wear the *hijab* created strong resistance among middle- and upper-class women in the major urban centers (Tabari and Yeganeh, 1982). This opposition movement, like many others, was eventually suppressed and the grip of *hijab* became harsher and stronger.

With the move to cover women came a concerted effort to return working women, particularly those in the civil service, to their homes. A campaign of harassment, purges, mandatory retirement, or monetary incentives for husbands of housewives made it extremely difficult, particularly in the early years of the revolution, for women to continue to work. Since then, the women's question has been a major issue, and at times a headache, for the new republic.

While the leaders share some general ideas about the place of women in Islamic society, they are far from united. Particularly in more recent years, a divergence of views is more apparent.[1]

It is imperative to point out that while government policies concern all women, the regime has paid particular attention to urban middle-class women. This is the group who was better positioned to take advantage of the Shah's reforms (Moghadam, 1988). Therefore, the current regime has targeted it more specifically as deviating from Islamic principles (Rafsanjani, 1990).

What are these principles? How have middle-class Iranian women deviated from them? Here again, close observation reveals that beneath an apparent unity there are conflicting approaches. The united front is primarily concerned with the place of women in the society, which subsequently defines their role. The zealots, who at the early stages defined a program of action, prefer a completely sex-segregated society in which women are relegated to the private sphere and men reign in the public, with one exception: women are needed in the streets to defend the revolution, denounce imperialism, and rally against any opposition. In an ideal situation, middle-class women would have abandoned their positions in the formal labor market and responded when called upon by the leaders. Referring to figure 2, women would be permanently engaged in the C area and temporarily in some overlap areas.

The regime has recognized that a completely sex-segregated society, though desired by some elements, is not practical. Policies have varied due to political and economic exigencies over time.

1. Economic necessities have made women an important part of the labor force. While women were systematically purged from the civil service, it proved impossible to remove them altogether from government jobs. Later some of those who were removed from the judiciary, higher education, and media were invited to return.

2. Young pro-regime women with a high school education replaced the purged professionals. This action itself created two unforeseen consequences. Many of these women, though loyal, were blatantly unqualified for their positions. Second, those who managed to maintain their positions, while supporting the regime's basic premises about women's role, became weary of the zealots' effort to exclude and degrade women and expressed dismay at some of the government's actions. [2]

3. Despite pressures, economic incentives, and harsh treatment, many women refused to leave their work and return home (Moghadam, 1988). Harassments were not limited to mixed environments; even in all-women environments, like schools, working women faced abuse by pro-regime elements. Nevertheless, many stayed. Their reasons varied from economic need to professional fulfillment or even resistance against the regime.[3]

Women have found various ways of resisting the regime, and the government's continuous obsession with women's behavior in public suggests that they have met with less than absolute compliance. Many middle-class women refused to return to the private domain and more are entering the job market in recent years.

The discourse of modesty among Muslim fundamentalists fluctuates with their respective position in the public domain. One can propose a positive relationship between the group's public difficulties and its imposed restrictions in the private domain. Those feeling vulnerable in the public domain are more likely to reinforce female modesty (see McCarthy Brown, 1994).

Islamic fundamentalist organizations' or governments' stands on women's issues are a product of their commitment to enforcement of *Shariat* and their political exigencies. The circumstances of the latter modifies the actuality of the former. The history of the Islamic Republic, the only fundamentalist state, reaffirms this premise. The gender discourse has evolved considerably in the republic. From calls to restore honor and defend Islam by returning women to the home and labeling uncooperative women as whores or lackeys of imperialism to calls for women to engage in world affairs reflects the institutionalization of fundamentalism. The early leaders envisioned a state that would withstand the imperialist threat, a hegemonic faith that would subdue the infidels, and a family that would control woman and protect man's honor.

This tripolar system was founded on strict adherence to Islam. The realization came early that if Islam were to be the founding base of the state, a significant degree of *ijtihad* (reinterpretation) was necessary. While the system still claims to be Islamic and is more so than other such-labeled governments, it is a far cry from what the Ayatollah perceived possible. Some of these realizations happened to the Ayatollah himself, for example, when in his first week of return from exile, he ordered electricity to be freely provided to everyone! Some came later. The state is still experimenting, and heated debates precede each step away from Islamic fundamentalism.

This *ijtihad* has taken a long while and is coming slowly to the private domain. Gradually, laws banning women from jobs,

education, public spaces, and particularly restrictions of their
family rights are being revised to fit the practical realities of the
modern world. The revolutionary macho fundamentalism has
gradually become urbane and sophisticated. There are
considerable historical, political, and economic reasons for this
transformation.

Among the historical events and social realities are the
death of the Ayatollah, the end of the war with Iraq, the Persian
Gulf War, and the unpopularity of supporting fundamentalist
movements abroad. The economic pressure and international
blockade have led to the realization that imperialism is perhaps
easy to defeat on the battleground, but difficult to tame in the
marketplace. The realities of participating in the capitalist world
market has toned down this fundamentalism in the public
domain, which in turn has affected its behavior in the private
domain in two ways: Directly, capitalism's demand for
maximum utilization of cheap labor has deterred a segregated
labor market. A reserved army of unemployed or even priv-
ileged workers is inefficient and unprofitable. So women's labor,
whether in white-collar jobs for teaching children or in the field
and sweatshops, is necessary. Indirectly and inevitably,
concessions in the public domain are trickling down to the
private domain, though in piecemeal fashion, inconsistently or
incoherently.

Another reason is the growing number of women who
matured during the revolution and are finding their voice in the
regime. These women are a product of the regime's educational
system, with its heavy Islamic rhetoric. They champion Islamic
doctrine but retain a claim to a "visible" place in the republic due
to their sacrifices and the support they have given the regime. It
is this group that can truly be labeled as Islamic feminists.

Though they will reject the label, their efforts on behalf of
women's rights are undeniable. Unlike the fundamentalist
groups elsewhere, in Iran, the Islamic feminists are inside the
system and not part of an opposition. Secular feminism is weak
and has no voice inside the country. In Iran, it is the state that
tries to redeem some of its previous extreme actions. This is in
response to the demand of feminists, both men and women, who
have realized the injustices of the past or sense a better

environment for criticism and reform. A majority of them are concentrated in the state. State reforms face opposition from the *Majles,* which is more responsive to conservative forces, particularly the lower middle class and rural populations. In the republic, the *Majles* is populist and the state is pragmatic.

Public relations and criticism from abroad have also reached the state officials, who are more in contact with the outside world than the *Majles'* deputies. Even there, women deputies are demanding revision of archaic laws regarding polygamy or have been trying to establish a special committee on women. In Iran, the dialogue is between Islamic feminists and fundamentalists. The secular feminists inside the country, by just surviving in the regime and through their presence in the civil service, have a contentious though silent effect.

In cases like Egypt and Pakistan, where fundamentalists are in opposition, the dialogue is between secular feminists and the fundamentalists (Badran, 1994; Mumtaz, 1994). The state responds to the group with stronger pressure, namely the fundamentalists. It compromises on women and family issues and coerces on political issues. For instance, the Sadat government compromised on his women's rights decree but never on the Camp David Accord or the Intifath policies. Mr. Mubarak is pursuing a similar approach. The appeasement of the opposition often comes at women's expense. As one example, Nawal El Saawadi, the well-known Egyptian activist and author, was detained and her last book was banned in 1991. In 1991, the vice governor of Cairo banned the Arab Women Solidarity Association headed by El Saawadi and allowed an auction of the association's property by an Islamic women's group headed by a man (Women Living Under Muslim Laws, 1991a).

President Zia ul-Hag of Pakistan instituted *chador,* the long scarf, and imposed restrictions on women's presence in higher education in 1980, while actively courting foreign investors and supporting American deeds in the Afghanistan war (Mumtaz, 1994). The Islamic Republic responds the same way. Female modesty, cultural invasion, or Westoxication are concerns of Islamic fundamentalism in the private domain. With every compromise in the public domain comes a surge in reinforcement of private domain fundamentalism. A joke in the streets of Tehran relates that whenever they (government) crack down on bad *hijabis*, they have made a deal with the foreigners (Westerners). The discourse of modesty is manipulated by states' desire to appease their opposition.

In societies in which public opinion is sensed rather than measured, women's participation in any social issue is hard to chart. Their voices come through, rarely directly, such as those of Islamic feminists, but mostly indirectly. Muffled voices relaying the pains of polygamy, divorce, abandonment, and other psychological or physical abuses, as reflected in women's letters to magazines and papers, in court cases, and references to government offices, are gradually and very slowly being heard. It is rare to have a direct response from masses of women. Even then, official, unofficial and even individual censorship forms the responses and the results.

In this study, I had a unique opportunity to gauge women's views regarding their social status during an important stage in the republic's life. The survey for this research was conducted in the summer of 1989, shortly after the signing of the cease-fire agreement with Iraq and immediately after the Ayatollah's death. These two historical events, followed by other changes, signaled the beginning of the end of the revolution and the start of the institutionalization process.

Iranian Women Respond

In this chapter answers to following questions are explored:
1. Do Iranian women perceive a functional duality of sex roles?

    (The extent of overlaps between these demarcations)
2. Do Iranian women see a spatial segregation of sexes?

    (The extent of their support for sex segregation)
3. How do Iranian women see their relation to power?

    (The extent of women's power in the family and society)
4. What are Iranian women's responses to feminism?

    (The extent of their support for sexual equality)

Research Design

A questionnaire with four scales was developed in Farsi and English. Two scales deal specifically with woman's place versus her role. Another scale measures women's perception of power and power management. The last scale measures group consciousness and the extent of support for feminist issues.

Previous studies have clearly indicated that Islamic fundamentalism is a middle and lower middle class phenomenon. In the initial stages of the revolution, all strata of middle-class urban women participated in the movement. Supporters of Islamic fundamentalism came mostly from the middle or lower middle classes (Tabari, 1982; Betteridge, 1983). Additionally, during the Pahlavi regime educational and occupational opportunities were concentrated in the large urban centers where middle-class women were better situated to take advantage of them. They were also better informed to benefit from legal reforms. At the time of the revolution, working women were present in government and business offices in the large cities. To the leaders of the revolution, this group symbolized decadence and the usurpation of Islamic principles of the patriarchal family and seclusion. They became the target of a widespread campaign of coercion and intimidation to enforce the new order. Thus, it was reasonable to concentrate on the middle-class women in urban areas.

Participants

During the summer of 1989, a Farsi version of the questionnaire was administered to a sample of female students in two universities in Tehran. Additionally, a leading women's magazine, *Zan-e-Rouz*, agreed to publish the questionnaire for their readers to complete and return (Gerami, 1989). The result was a national sample of 1,098 responses, of which 103 were completed by men. Due to the small number of this group, their responses are not included here. The total number of completed questionnaires by women are 854, of which 54 percent are from Tehran, 20 percent from other major cities, 12 percent from small towns, and the rest unspecified. This is not a random sample, but when compared to characteristics of middle-class women in urban areas as reported in the 1986 national census, this group comes very close to being representative of middle-class women (Statistical Center, 1987). Furthermore, means and standard errors calculated for all variables indicate a probability of .05 that this sample may not be within a 95 percent range of the population mean.

Table 5.1 presents a summary of participants' characteristics. The majority of respondents were students, followed by housewives, which leaves about 40 percent of the sample as either full-time or part-time employed. In terms of education, 80 percent of respondents had high school or less than high school education. Some 13 percent reported college and higher education. Generally, this sample was young, single or married with small families, and high school educated. Among those who were employed, the largest number were teachers, civil service employees, and secretaries.

Questionnaire items are divided into four scales, with tables presenting descriptive statistics.

TABLE 5.1. GENERAL CHARACTERISTICS
OF THE IRANIAN SAMPLE (%) [*]

Employment		Yrs Employ[†]		Education		Marital		# Children		Age	
Ft	16.0	1-5	47.7	< Hs	33.7	M	41.4	1-2	22.9	> 20	31.4
Pt	7.0	6-10	20.1	Hs	47.0	S	57.2	3-4	10.9	21-30	50.9
Hsw	22.8	11-15	13.8	2 Cl	6.3	W	.7	5-7	1.3	31-40	11.6
Ret	5.5	16-20	7.8	Cl	11.8	D	.7	None	64.8	41-50	5.3
Std	36.0	>20	10.6	> Cl	1.2					>50	5
Unem	11.2										

Key: Ft = Full Time , Pt = Part Time, Hsw = Housewife, Ret = Retired,
       Std = Student, Unem = Unemployed, Hs = High School, Cl = College,
       M=Married, S=Single, W=Widowed, D=Divorced

This table does not include missing cases.

[*] Means and standard errors for the variables indicate that the probability that this sample is not within the 95 percent range of the population is >.05.

[†] Not including students and housewives.

Feminine/Masculine Functions

A scale with seven items measured attitudes toward woman's proper role. Table 5.2 presents an English translation of the items with descriptive statistics for the scale. As the means and standard deviations show, there is some consistency among respondents with regard to woman's proper place. Two questions in particular, dealing with the primacy of the man's occupation and the wife's responsibility to support his job (items one and two), show that women agree on the greater importance of a man's job compared to a woman's job. They also agree that their primary function is motherhood. This does not, however, suggest that they should remain out of the formal job market. An overwhelming majority of 93 percent believe that a woman should emphasize her work as much as her husband's job (item three). The next three questions show clear support for the functional duality of feminine versus masculine occupations. Question four with a mean of 1.54 and standard deviation of .84 confirms the above idea. Therefore, masculine occupations, such as mechanics, are not suitable for women (item five), while teaching is more compatible with her "nature" (item six).

TABLE 5.2. WOMEN'S FUNCTION INDEX

		Mean	Median	Stdev
1.	Woman give up her job interfere family	1.6	1.0	1.94
2.	Men's job to bring money, women's is family	2.25	2.0	1.09
3.	Woman should emphasize her job as much as his	1.29	1.0	.67
4.	Job suit her femininity	1.54	1.0	.84
5.	Carpentry, mechanics not women's job	1.57	1.0	.98
6.	Best occupation for women is teaching	2.27	2.0	1.11
7.	Women have easier life	3.39	4.0	.90

So far, this index supports some of the Islamic Republic's policies of sex-role allocation, which recognizes and elevates motherhood and housekeeping as woman's primary responsibilities. The next question is: Are women happy with their current status? This, of course, cannot be specifically and openly addressed in a general questionnaire. Item seven is designed to provide some indication of women's satisfaction with their status. Tables 5.2 and 5.3 fail to show that women consider their lives easier than men's. Indeed, over 81 percent reject this notion. If ambiguities of modern values during the previous regime created discontent (Fischer, 1978), promoting a traditional role for women has not created satisfaction with their roles.

TABLE 5.3. WOMEN'S FUNCTION: % DISTRIBUTION

		SA	AS	DS	SD
1.	Woman give up her job interfere family	63.6	20.5	7.7	8.2
2.	Men's job is to bring money, women's is family	31.3	31.2	18.3	19.2
3.	Woman should emphasize her job as his	80.1	12.7	4.7	2.5
4.	Job suit her femininity	63.0	25.4	6.1	5.5
5.	Carpentry, mechanics not women's job	69.4	13.6	7.5	9.4
6.	Best occupation for women is teaching	30.3	33.0	15.3	21.4
7.	Women have easier life	5.2	13.4	19.2	62.3

Key: SA = Strongly Agree, AS = Agree Somewhat, DS = Disagree Somewhat, SD= Strongly Disagree.

Private/Public Spheres

Another scale with six questions was designed to measure women's attitudes toward spatial segregation of the sexes. As Tables 5.5 and 5.6 show, item eight, with a mean of 1.63 and standard deviation of .88, indicates that 86 percent believe women's happiness is inside the home regardless of her achievements in the outside world. This reaffirms the findings of the previous scale that housekeeping and motherhood are perceived as women's primary functions and home as their primary domain. But, while agreeing on their primary functions, women reject restrictions on their options in terms of role and place. They overwhelmingly reject the idea that working women are unfeminine (item nine). The majority do not believe that women should stay out of the job market to open up jobs for men (item ten), or that girls' education should be limited to training for mothering (item eleven), or that happiness for girls is in marriage and for boys is in education. In other words, women do not see any contradiction in combining their traditional roles with other opportunities. Mothering should not limit their other options. Taken together, the results of items nine to eleven display women's rejection of spatial seclusion.

TABLE 5.4. WOMEN'S FUNCTION: CORRELATION MATRIX

	1	2	3	4	5	6	7
1		.27*	.10*	.32*	.22*	.21*	.14*
2			-.02	.27*	.21*	.30*	.10*
3				.01*	.06	.10*	.05
4					.35*	.31*	.10*
5						.17*	.16*
6							.14*
7							

* $P = <.05$.

TABLE 5.5. WOMEN'S PLACE INDEX

		Mean	Median	Stdev
8.	Women's happiness, homemaking, regardless of her achievement outside	1.63	1.0	.88
9.	Want outside job unfeminine	3.32	3.0	.95
10.	High unemployment, women stay home	2.73	3.0	1.15
11.	Girl ed suitable roles: mother and housewife	2.87	3.0	1.16
12.	Boys' happiness ed, girls' marriage	3.33	4.0	.98
13.	Proud husband dislikes wife to work	2.67	3.0	1.09

According to both custom and Islamic scripture, men are the guardians of women, both spiritually and physically. A man's honor is closely linked to the behavior of his womenfolk. To safeguard their honor, men prefer to seclude women (Abu-Laughod, 1986). Question thirteen directly asks women if proud husbands dislike their wives to work. A mean of 2.67 shows that a slight majority of 54 percent report moderate disagreement with this idea. But a standard deviation of 1.09 also points out that women are not clear about men's preference. The small number of men who responded to this questionnaire were also divided. The result indicates moderate disapproval of this proposal.

TABLE 5.6. WOMEN'S PLACE: % DISTRIBUTION

		SA	AS	DS	SD
8.	Women's happiness, homemaking, regardless of her achievement outside	56.9	29.4	7.2	6.6
9.	Want outside job unfeminine	4.8	20.1	13.5	61.6
10.	High unemployment, women stay home	19.9	23.9	19.3	36.9
11.	Girl ed suitable roles: mother and housewife	71.1	23.0	15.5	44.4
12.	Boys' happiness ed, girls' marriage	7.5	14.5	15.7	62.3
13.	Proud husband dislikes wife to work	17.5	28.6	23.6	30.4

TABLE 5.7. WOMEN'S PLACE: CORRELATION MATRIX

	8	9	10	11	12	13
8		.06	$.16^*$	$.21^*$	$.16^*$	$.10^*$
9			$.16^*$	$.21^*$	$.19^*$	$.13^*$
10				$.22^*$	$.18^*$	$.14^*$
11					$.30^*$	$.14^*$
12						$.14^*$
13						

$^* P = <.05.$

Comparing the results of these indexes, sex-role specialization receives stronger support than spatial segregation. Practical reality also supports these findings. After a short decline immediately after the revolution, women's labor force participation has increased consistently (Moghadam, 1993). In 1990, the ratio of female to male postsecondary enrollment was 39, and the percentage of women in the economically active population was 18 (Khalidi and Tucker, 1992:4–5). Moghadam reports, "Women in the public sector tend to be largely professional, highly educated, salaried. They are found mainly in education and medicine. They are less likely to be married" (ibid.:196).

Women and Power

Another scale with seven items measured women's relation to power. This index treats three related issues with regard to women's power. Questions fourteen and fifteen seek information about women's general ideas regarding their ability to make decisions and handle power. Questions sixteen, seventeen, and eighteen measure practical applications of men's and women's power in the family. Items nineteen and twenty measure women's support for Islamic principles of female subordination. Tables 5.8 and 5.9 show the statistical summary of these results.

TABLE 5.8. WOMEN'S RELATION TO POWER INDEX

		Mean	Median	Stdev
14.	Women incapable of making important decisions	3.0	3.0	.96
15.	Men more capable to handle power	2.46	1.0	.88
16.	Women have real power at home	2.63	4.0	.90
17.	Father import. decisions for future children	3.01	3.0	.99
18.	Father should be guardian in divorce	3.50	4.0	.85
19.	Weaker psych = weaker mental/psych	3.69	4.0	.74
20.	No intellectual strength for judiciary/politics	3.02	3.0	1.05

TABLE 5.9. RELATION TO POWER: % DISTRIBUTION

		SA	AS	DS	SD
14.	Women incapable of making important decisions	5.6	30.1	21.6	42.6
15.	Men more capable to handle power	20.0	39.4	15.8	24.9
16.	Women have power at home	11.6	37.5	27.7	23.3
17.	Father import. decisions for future children	7.2	26.8	23.8	42.2
18.	Father should be guardian in divorce	5.3	7.4	19.3	68.0
19.	Weaker psych = weaker mental/psych	3.4	6.1	8.2	82.3
20.	No intellectual strength for judiciary/politics	11.5	19.7	23.9	44.9

Responses to items fourteen and fifteen seem to record contradictory messages. Participants reject the idea that women are incapable of making important decisions (item fouteen), but 60 percent of them believe that men are more capable of handling power than women. Other statistical measures of these two items (not shown here) indicate that women do not see these points as contradictory. Indeed, women reject the notion of being innately deficient but perceive inadequacy in power management.

Questions sixteen, seventeen, and eighteen provide an interesting picture of women's relation to power in the family by overwhelmingly rejecting men's unilateral power in deciding family matters. Shortly after the revolution, the new regime abrogated the Family Protection Law, enacted by the previous regime, and restored men's unilateral right to divorce and have custody of children. Question eighteen specifically asks women's opinion about this policy. According to statistics in tables 5.8 and 5.9, this item with a mean of 3.50, a standard deviation of .85, and a 6.6 proportion of agreement over disagreement reports women's unanimous disapproval of this policy.

TABLE 5.10. RELATION TO POWER:
CORRELATION MATRIX

	12	13	14	15	16	17	18
12		.46*	-.00	.21*	.22*	.35*	.40*
13			-.03	.22*	.26*	.25*	.34*
14				.05	.00	-.00	-.00
15					.25*	.12*	.15*
16						.21*	-.25*
17							.32*
18							

$^*P = <.05.$

Taken together, these four items suggest that at an abstract level women do not see themselves as power holders and decision makers. At the family level, they strongly reject their subservient position with regard to men's power.

Islamic literature contains references to woman's physical and mental weakness and her emotional instability. For these reasons, women are barred from the judiciary and some political positions, like the presidency. Questions nineteen and twenty specifically address these issues and are rejected. Some 92 percent of the respondents, with a mean of 3.69 and a standard deviation of .74, refute women's inherent intellectual inferiority. About 70 percent dispute women's intellectual inadequacy for politics and the judiciary. The difference between means of 3.69 for item nineteen and 3.02 for twenty could be due to the fact that since women are barred from these occupations in Iran, some respondents, addressing item twenty were stating the fact rather than their opinion. Many respondents wrote comments on their questionnaires. Male respondents who agreed with item twenty, often wrote statements such as "because of her emotional nature" in the margin. Female respondents who disagreed with this statement wrote comments such as "What about Mrs. Bhuto?" or "Nobody believes this anymore," or "Islam never said women are weak, it is misinterpreted." The results for this index are very similar to the one for the Egyptian sample.

1. Iranian women reject the idea that they are innately inadequate to handle power and make rational decisions.

2. They agree in general that they are neither competent power holders nor decision makers; thus, in practical matters they delegate decision making to men.

3. With regard to family matters, however, men's unilateral decision making does not receive women's support.

The middle-class Iranian women have not internalized the ideological foundation of male supremacy in Islam. On the political scene, they seem to concede power to men; this reluctant abdication of their rights does not, however, extend into family matters. Here, in practical matters, such as the future of children, women want their right to participate in decision making. One explanation is that respondents interpret power in political and administrative terms.

Feminism

A scale with seven items designed to gauge women's attitudes on feminist issues, ranging from financial and educational opportunities for women to solidarity and group consciousness, provides surprising results. Tables 5.11 and 5.12 show descriptive statistics and frequency distributions for each category.

TABLE 5.11. FEMINISM INDEX

		Mean	Median	Stdev
21.	Women can perform any job men can	2.32	2.0	.92
22.	Fair to expect husband to help with chores	1.63	1.0	.83
23.	Educational materials girls = boys	1.71	1.0	1.07
24.	Best for girls to marry early	3.48	4.0	.89
25.	Worst enemies of women other women	2.85	3.0	1.31
26.	Cannot trust a woman with a secret	2.9	3.0	.83
27.	Generally no solidarity among women	2.82	3.0	1.06

TABLE 5.12. FEMINISM: % DISTRIBUTION

		SA	AS	DS	SD
21.	Women can perform any job men can	19.2	41.5	27.4	11.9
22.	Fair to expect husband to help with chores	62.4	16.0	9.0	12.6
23.	Educational materials girls = boys	54.8	30.9	9.9	4.4
24.	Best for girls to marry early	5.5	10.6	14.1	69.8
25.	Worst enemies of women other women	16.6	23.0	19.6	40.8
26.	Cannot trust a woman with a secret	12.7	26.4	18.9	42.0
27.	Generally no solidarity among women	11.6	31.4	19.9	37.1

Two items measuring equalitarian relationships between the sexes in the family and society receive positive responses from the participants. The first item asks a general question about equality between the sexes. A mean of 2.32 and a standard deviation of 0.92 show that the majority support equality of sexes. Equalitarian relations in household responsibilities, measured by item twenty-two, also receives strong support from the respondents. Two items measure treatment for boys and girls in the family. Equality of education for boys and girls measured by item twenty-three is supported by 72 percent of the respondents. Similarly, early marriage of girls, measured by item twenty-four, is strongly rejected. Taken together, these items show that women support some aspects of gender equality at the family level.

Anthropological studies have recorded group support and cohesiveness among women in the extended family or community in Middle Eastern societies (Friedl, 1989). At the same time, traditional hostility among the in-laws and fear of polygamous marriage can lead to lack of trust and adversarial relations among women. This study also attempted to measure the degree of conscious support, reliance, and trust among women, and the extent to which practical behavior translates into a collective consciousness of solidarity with other women.

TABLE 5.13. FEMINISM: CORRELATION MATRIX

	21	22	23	24	25	26	27
21		.17*	.13*	-.14*	-.06	-.05	.00
22			.11*	-.10*	.01	-.01	.10*
23				-.61*	-.01	-.10*	.04
24					.20*	.17*	.11*
25						.37*	.26*
26							.38*
27							

* $P = <.05$.

The three items that are designed to measure group consciousness, trust, and solidarity suggest a moderate level of cognitive feminism. The majority of the sample (60 percent) reject adversarial relationships among women, measured by item twenty-five, with a mean of 2.85. They also dispute the statement in question twenty-six that women are not trustworthy, with a mean of 2.9. The last item, twenty-seven, with a mean of 2.82, relates a moderate degree of solidarity among the sample. Since all of these means are within the 95 percent range of population mean, one can detect some level of cognitive solidarity among the middle-class urban women of Iran.

Retesting Some Old Hypotheses

It is suggested that women's socioeconomic status affects their degree of feminism, acceptance of gender equality, and in general their perception of sex roles (Klatch, 1988). A series of analyses of variance were conducted to measure the degree of association between respondents' education, occupation, marital status, age, place of residence, and the four indexes tested here. The results are presented in table 5.14.

TABLE 5.14. ANALYSIS OF VARIANCE

	Function	Place	Power	Feminism
Education	38.39	72.85	16.5	12.58
	$P=.03$	$P=.01$	$P=.2$	$P=.3$
Employment	89.40	500.0	126.8	.008
	$P=.00$	$P=.00$	$P=.00$	$P=.9$
Marital	41.92	298.0	92.58	6.77
	$P=.02$	$P=.00$	$P=.00$	$P=.4$
Age	4.46	34.03	34.57	28.9
	$P=.3$	$P=.9$	$P=.1$	$P=.1$
Residence	9.95	.95	110.0	24.0
	$P=.5$	$P=.9$	$P=.01$	$P=.36$

This procedure treats each status variable, such as education, as an independent variable and tests its effect on each dependent variable, for instance, respondents' attitude toward their role. A statistically significant relationship allows generalization from the sample to the population, suggesting that the same relationship exists in the population. As table 5.14 shows, education influences women's perception of their proper role and place. It fails, however, to show a significant relationship with women's relation to power and their feminist consciousness. Considering the youth and moderate education of this sample, lack of relationship between education and feminist consciousness challenges others' findings.

Women's employment status influences their perception of feminine and masculine functions and their attitudes toward spatial restriction. It also positively contributes to a sense of empowerment, ANOVA=200. As far as feminism is concerned, employment shows no relationship with feminist consciousness.

A surprising result is the significant contribution of marital status to women's perception of sex roles. Analysis of variance between marital status and attitudes toward functional duality reports a positive and strong relationship. A stronger ANOVA of 500 is observed between this status indicator and the place index. Marital status affects rejection of sex segregation. This variable also affects women's relation to power and their own empowerment. As in previous indicators, marital status shows no significant relationship with feminism.

Respondents' age also does not contribute to our understanding of variations in their attitudes. Given the general youth of this sample, this result is not surprising. Neither does place of residence further our understanding of their attitudes. The only significant relationship observed here is between place of residence and relation to power. Neither age nor residence relays significant relationship with feminist attitudes. Indeed, none of the status variables seems to affect women's degree of support for feminist issues. Feminism as measured here receives positive support from the sample. Nevertheless, neither education nor employment nor any other indicators of respondents' characteristics show any relationship with feminism.

Conclusion

The main objective of this research was to explore women's perception of spatial versus functional duality of sex roles within the context of Islamic fundamentalism in Iran. Are these theoretical constructs supported by women's cognitive recognition? The result shows that women identify functional duality to be more salient than spatial segregation. They clearly identify separate functions for men and women and recognize feminine functions as women's primary responsibilities. Recognizing that, they then reject restrictions on their opportunities in the job market. Spatial segregation as measured here is clearly rejected by the respondents.

With regard to the dichotomies, the findings identify four areas: (1) Woman's nurturing capacity dictates her familial obligation as her primary responsibility. (2) This responsibility is not grounds for her spatial seclusion. (3) Feminine occupations are recommended as women's outlet in the labor market. (4) Consequently, functional duality is recognized and approved more readily than spatial duality.

The result for women's relation to power and their capacity for rational judgment indicates two points: (a) rejection of women's intellectual inferiority; and (b) their belief in men's superior capacity to make important decisions and hold power. While there is some support for their reluctance to assume power, there is strong evidence that they believe men are better decision makers. One can conclude that women have not internalized the ideology rationalizing patriarchy, but have been socialized to accept it as practical.

As far as their power in the family is concerned, we have clear indication as to where women stand. The Islamic patriarchy, which defines man as the ultimate decision maker in the family, is challenged and rejected. It is important to point out that this study did not address the legitimacy of man as the head of household. Numerous interviews and contacts have convinced this observer that Iranian women do not question the authority of man as the head of household. Rather, these findings suggest that man's unilateral power is questioned and that woman's right in decision making at the family level is recognized.

With regard to feminism, three specific areas were measured: gender equality at the family level, group consciousness, and group solidarity. As measured here, middle-class Iranian women display a substantial degree of feminism by supporting familial gender equality, group consciousness, and group solidarity. This did not vary with the respondents' education or employment (not shown here). It can be due to the fact that feminism as measured here is so universally of concern to women and so elementary that women in Iran, regardless of their education and employment, support these basic rights. The experience of participating in the revolution can also foster a sense of solidarity and support for basic equal rights of the sexes.

Finally, overshadowed by attention to the antiwomen rhetoric of the regime, efforts of enlightened clergy and women activists inside the regime are obscured. They promote women's rights within the framework of Islamic doctrine presenting women as competent and dignified members of the *ummat* (community). Woman's role delineated by her reproductive capacity is focused around the family and supportive services to men's activities. This type of feminism emphasizes "relational" female identity and focuses on a functional sex-role model, which to some extent also delineates each sex's place in the society (International Institute for Adult Literacy, undated). All of these contribute to support for women's equal rights in the family and a sense of common bonds and shared interest.

In sum, the middle-class Iranian women who participated in the Islamic revolution have not internalized the social identity that the republic has decreed them. Despite fifteen years of mass propaganda and restrictive policies, they reaffirm their right to occupy the public space as they choose. This clearly shows that a sex-segregated ideal society envisioned by the revolutionary leaders has failed to enlist the middle-class women's support. While the state's Islamic rhetoric has reaffirmed their belief in complementary sex roles in society and family, it has failed to justify men's right to dictate women's public behavior. This study investigates women's response to an ideal Islamic society, promised by the revolution, in which women know their proper place. Women have clearly declared that their place is where they choose it to be, not where it is decreed to be.

NOTES

1. In December of 1990, while President Rafsanjani cautioned against harsh reaction to prohibited acts, the zealots were establishing a new vice unit to fight symbols of Westernization and bad *Hijabi, Iran Times*, 43:16.

Bad *hijabi* refers to any deviation from strict Islamic standards from colorful *hijabis* to boutique windows displaying women's clothing.

2. Ms. Rahnavard denounced the recent crackdowns on bad *hijabis, Iran Times*, 1990, 11:1.

3. During the summer of 1989, I interviewed thirty-eight professional women about their family and occupational status in Tehran.

CHAPTER SIX

Iranian Women Leaders Speak about Family, Power, and Feminism

Introduction

Since the beginning of the revolution, a group of women, either through their own action or by extension of their male relatives, have remained with the revolution and the Republic. Some have gained offical leadership positions, some have de facto power and no official title. Like similar fundamentalist movements, the top leadership in the republic has been all male. Below this group, there is a group of women sprinkled throughout the power structure of the state bureacracy or its affiliated institutions. Some are well known due to their positions or their personalities, some remain behind the scene unknown to the public. Despite their official titles, they affect state policies in general and women issues in particular. This chapter reports the results of a series of interviews with thirty-eight women leaders and three target group discussions.

Selection Process and Participants' Characteristics

The data for this part were collected in 1989 and 1992. Most of the interviews and focus group discussions took place in 1989. Five members of the original sample of the leaders were interviewed again in 1992, and three new leaders were added. Of the original group, three who were dependent on men for their status have lost most of their power though remaining public figures. These women were tied to the conservative faction, which was defeated in the 1992 election.

The interviewees were selected based on reputation and availability. Some women had official positions and others enjoyed a public profile. Among the latter, many had no official title, and their public exposure was due to their husband's or other male relative's status. These women had successfully utilized men's positions and had gained public exposure and, in some cases, public office. The wife of the ex-speaker of the house who is in charge of the Shahid Institution's hospitals, the largest chain of hospitals in the country, is of the second category. She has maintained her position and power despite setbacks suffered by her husband.

What universally came through was that these women had sought and chosen to be public and enjoyed the power of their positions. Some had personal ambition and others used their resources to further women's causes. The wife of the ex-prime minister, Ms. Zahra Rahnavard, is the best-known advocate of women's rights in Iran. She managed to remove many quotas for women's admissions into the universities. She is also an artist in her own right.

Not all wives of leaders occupy a public life. Foremost among them is the wife of the Ayatollah Khomeini. An eloquent and efficient woman, she has shunned public office, while her daughter, Mrs. Mustafavi, who was interviewed for this research in 1989, is the president of the Women's Society (the state's women's organization). After her father's death and the new *Majles* in 1992, Mrs. Mostafavi has lost some of her power. She and her brother stand slightly to the right of the present government.

In collecting my list, most participants, either voluntarily or in response to my request, proposed other names and produced telephone numbers. Generally, those who held office and had higher educational background were more open and less hesitant about interviews. Some allowed the interview to be taped. Others were very concerned about expressing their views and emphasized that they do not want to be misquoted. Members of this group were more likely to be related to a male official.

The majority of the subjects came from either clergy or *bazzari* (merchant) families. Twenty-one had solid middle or upper middle class backgrounds. The rest came from lower middle class families. Eighty-seven percent had a college degree, 12 percent had traditional theological training, and one was from a peasant background.

In addition to this group, three focus group discussions were organized: one with college students and teachers, one with women activists, and one composed of professionals and housewives. Finally, informal conversations with men and women of different backgrounds provided additional data for this chapter.

I have organized these interviews around the four themes of this book: women's role, women's place, women and power, and gender equality.

The span of three years has made a significant qualitative change in Iran. Among the historical events are

- death of the revolution's leader, Ayatollah Khomeini;
- end of the eight-year-long war with Iraq;
- gradual consolidation of power in the hands of President Rafsanjani and his faction known in the West as "the pragmatists";
- release of Western hostages from Lebanon;
- improved relations with Western countries;
- economic improvements;
- liberalization of social mores;
- an aggressive population control campaign;
- and, of special interest here, grass roots efforts by women to improve their educational, occupational, and social opportunities.

These and other changes had led to a marked difference in the most conservative women leaders' attitude toward women's rights and choices in the Islamic Republic. They had adjusted their definition of woman's nature—psyche and physique—to a more modern interpretation. Instead of just praising Islam's treatment of women, they advocated more legal protection. There was more criticism of the system and its shortcomings as far as granting women their true Islamic rights were concerned. The leaders, nevertheless, unlike the focus groups, defended the system and universally had some criticism of the Western societies' treatment of women. Among the latter, an American-educated psychologist put forth the most orthodox interpretation of the Islamic doctrine while attacking Western ways.

Functional Duality

"You women who work outside [home] as physicians, professors, planners or other practical occupations, these are important in their own rights, but keep in mind the home front" (Ayatollah Khaamenie, 1992). The Islamic Republic's rhetoric abounds with woman as mother and care giver. The message reverberating throughout the country is that the Islamic Republic has granted woman her whole personhood, which was neglected by the previous regime. The Shah's regime made woman into a toy or sex object. This came across in several interviews. A female law consultant said, "Woman was only a beauty symbol. Women are half of the society and must be active participants."

The importance of woman's reproductive function is integral to her individual and social identity. To remove the former destroys the latter. This goes beyond Islamic culture, and it is interwoven into Iranian culture that any definition of "self" for woman is directly and causally linked to her reproductive capacity (see Gerami, 1993).

In interviews with an official paper, wives of the officials in the Islamic Republic unanimously declared that a woman should engage in the social arena if it does not detract from her major responsibility as a wife and mother. A more orthodox view is expressed by the wife of a well-known clergyman:

> Women must be obedient and have knowledge about women's issues and know techniques of housekeeping and if she is obliged to engage in outside activities, she must know how to manage household. Women must perform motherhood, which is one of the most important responsibilities of women, excellently. A woman must understand her husband and children easily. During our 26 years of married life with that great martyr, I tried to be

obedient and submissive, because he was in higher plateau of religious devotion. (*Havai*, 1988:6)

She represents the ultraconservative view of women's social role. Interestingly, a female dermatologist expressed similar views in a focus group discussion. Her conservative view of women's role was not based on Islam but on women's nature. She disapproved of male nurses in the hospital where she worked. Describing how she observed a male nurse feeding an infant, she stated, "It looked very unnatural. Men shouldn't be nurses and I told him so." A teacher described the social pressure women face to comply with expected roles: "After you get married, gossip starts about why she is not pregnant. Family members, especially the husband's family, wonder if you are sterile. Finally, your husband submits and tells you to get pregnant and stay home to stop the rumors."

If women questioned the time of motherhood, or frequency of child bearing, or whether to combine work and family, no one questioned the choice of motherhood. The director of a government-funded research center on women's issues, an American-trained psychologist, stated: "Marriage and motherhood is a woman's primary responsibility. Freedom in Islam is different from the West. In Islam a woman cannot remain single, it is not a sin, but not encouraged. A woman must emphasize her motherhood and household responsibilities."

Among the women leaders, whether following the official line or expressing their personal views, the majority maintained that woman's primary responsibility is motherhood and housekeeping. This is grounded in the nature-based idea of woman's personality. "She has a delicate spirit and is sensitive, she is naturally emotional," a director of an educational institution stated. A female lawyer stated:

> Every person has a nature at the time of creation. Women have certain characteristics. Men have more physical strength and are accordingly responsible for hard tasks. Part of the difference is due to the creation. Delicate and sensitive tasks are assigned to women and men are responsible for financial support of the family.

The female physician disapproved of women as surgeons or any type of medicine dealing with emergency cases. She related a story of a female anesthesiologist who, one night, was picked up at her house by two other doctors, both male, for an emergency operation during the war. "It was this young woman in the car with two men at the middle of night." She related, "Men were unhappy about this situation too. One of them said 'if you women stayed out of medical schools more men could attend and we would not have to drag women doctors out of their homes at the middle of the night.'"

A high school math teacher and wife of a *Majles* deputy put it most clearly:

> Women's occupation should suit their physical and psychological condition; at the same time it should not be harmful to the family and children. I believe the best occupation for women is teaching, which in Islam is recommended, too. Meanwhile, Islam has no restriction on women's occupation and they can engage in all areas whether technical, medical, political, economics, and even in higher occupational positions involved in decision making of the society. Of course, on rare occasions there are some restrictions which are for her own good and are mostly customary. For instance, mining reduces woman's energy and detracts from her main responsibility which is motherhood and housekeeping, it is not suitable for women. If women's occupations are like men's, inflexible, undoubtedly, it hurts women. Therefore, we see that all around the world, women seek social justice, to be able to take care of their main responsibility which is motherhood. (*Kayhan Havai*, 1988:7)

This idea is reflected in the official policy, which reduces the workweek, allows ninety days paid maternity leave, a thirty-minute break every three hours for nursing mothers, on-site day care, as well as other benefits indicated in the new labor law.

Women as public figures generally recited the official line about the importance of motherhood and led an active public life. They were quick to mention that they do not shortchange their families. The principal of an educational institution (kindergarten to twelfth grade) repeatedly mentioned that she manages her five children beautifully and works twelve hours a day at her job.

The younger women participating in discussion groups advocated individual choice and downplayed the role of feminine nature. One group discussion took place in the office of a women's opposition group. This association is organized by the daughter of a leading theologian and an opposition leader to the Shah's regime. He and most of his family experienced prison and persecution. A devout Muslim, his daughter is to the left of the government. Her office, in addition to publishing a monthly newspaper, offers classes for women and legal counseling. Most participants in our two sessions were young and from working-class families. Their major concern was to maximize their resources. Of the nineteen participants, all but two had a high school diploma, but college was not part of their future.

We met in the society's main office in central Tehran in a building that used to be the Saudi Arabian embassy. It is a grand old building with open and airy rooms. The young women participants were active in a variety of community work and were critical of the government. They were enrolled in classes in typing, computers, sewing, etc. Their priorities were to find a suitable husband who has a stable job and is moderately supportive, to be able to work for at least the first few years of their marriage, and to avoid living with in-laws. In one of our two sessions, they had a heated debate about women's nature. Surprisingly, they were well versed in the nature versus nurture debate. However, they took a pragmatic view toward their roles and future. At the end of our first meeting, when we were all putting our various *hijabs* on, a tall cheerful-looking woman said, "I don't care what they [government] say about women [self] sacrificing for everybody else. I control my destiny." She winked. "I want two kids, a two-bedroom apartment, and a good job, and I am not going to sacrifice it."

It is imperative to mention that the state's definition of women and their status is dynamic and forming rather than static and decided. Women have been important players in the debate. A brief overview indicates that a trend toward liberalization is occurring. In a speech to the Social and Cultural Council of Women, the religious leader advocated an increase in

the number of female physicians, proportional to their population (Khaamenie, 1992:7, 86).

Spatial Separation

"Women botanists who conduct research in our institution are
not allowed to travel, so for their research materials they rely on
vegetations collected by untrained men" (*Zan-e-Rouz*, 1992:10).

The answer to the question Should women remain
segregated from men? is generally No. Even the most
conservative do not prescribe the complete seclusion of women.
However, when the definition of seclusion is sought, the answer
is less clear.

When it comes to segregation, attention to its scope, extent,
and dimension is necessary. While all women and men with
whom I talked rejected a ban on women's participation in the
labor market, views on the extent of gender integration varied
with age, social class, and family background of the
interviewees. A general consensus among the women leaders
indicated that women, after administering to their families, can
and should engage in outside activities. All agreed that women
deserve special provisions in order to participate in the labor
market. Meanwhile, they advocated equal pay for equal work.

Disagreement surfaced when the type of participation and
circumstances of participation were debated. Therefore, the
public versus private debate needs to expand the definition
beyond mere spatial dimension and include behavioral
segregation. The controversial national debate about *hijab*,
malhijabi, or good *hijabi* denotes one aspect of this segregation.
Many areas of public space are segregated: sports stadiums are
men's domain, as are the upper deck of double-decker buses, the
front seat of buses, the front rows of classrooms on college
campuses, and so forth. However, *hijab* has implications far
beyond mere geographical dimension. It has redefined a public
and personal space that did not exist to this extent in the Iranian
culture.

The Islamic *hijab* is more than a dress code, it is a live and
dynamic social ethic that includes a set of values and norms of
interaction. A civil service employee stated that in 1979, after the

revolution, women could not laugh in the workplace. Now it has changed, but women still should not smoke in public. She stated that she was told not to cross her legs because it arouses men.

The Islamic dress code can be divided into three categories, with each denoting a particular ideological and political view as well as social class and status. Each category has nuances and details in which the experienced eye can detect individualism, resistance, rejection, commitment, devotion, and fashion, as well as social status. The same symbolism exists in American culture, though to a lesser extent. I was reminded of this when I tried to explain women's dress and fashion statements and their implied symbolism to my sister who was visiting the United States for the first time in 1990.

To begin with, the Islamic *hijab* required by many offices and schools consists of a long and loose robe of heavy and dark colored material called *"mantu"* (from French *manteau*). A pair of pants or dark and heavy stockings, flat shoes, and a head cover that covers all of a woman's hair complete this ensemble. It is the choice of the latter that draws the boundaries of segregation, ideology, and social standing.

Head covers are generally of three kinds. The generic head cover required as part of the official dress code is called *"maghnae."* It is headgear that is sewn with an opening for the face. It does not require any fastening or ties, thus it is more functional and easier to manage than a head scarf, which requires continuous adjustment to cover all strands of hair. Made mostly of heavy and dark materials, it is uncomfortable in Iran's hot summers. This is mandatory in offices and schools. In government offices, one is well advised to wear *maghnae* instead of a scarf. I learned quickly that in offices or when interviewing government officials, it is the cover of choice.

When attired as such, only a woman's face and hands will show. Maghnae is the middle ground of the head covers. One can detect a woman's ideological support for the system, depending on the rest of her ensemble.

A *mantu* and *maghnae* (MM) of generic description implies following the rule and not shaking the boat. This woman is very likely not an Islamic ideologue and is too busy with work and family to tamper with the official dress code. She most likely works outside the home and is coming or going to her work.

To the left of this category are those who wear a head scarf, called "*rusary*" (instead of *maghnae*), which is tied around the neck and over a *mantu*. This ensemble, called "*mantu va rusary*" (MR), denotes a nonadvocate and even opposition to the system. This group is more relaxed outside the official domain. Their attire varies from expensive, elegant, and fashionable to, at times, tacky. The author met a teenager who, during the difficult days of 1985 when the war and bombing raged, wore a baby-blue *rusary* so masterfully around her head and neck that it left her earlobes exposed to show her fashionable earrings. She, of course, was playing with the wrath of the morality squads who roamed the street in search of deviants from the strictest dress codes.

MR is patterned and designed so that it can express individuality by experimenting with the texture and design of the outfit. Given the authorities' reaction against jeans, any form of denim expresses fashion and opposition. Since a woman's hair should not be shown in public, attempts are made to display strands of hair somehow or another. One way, as practiced between 1989 and 1992, was showing strands of hair, often bleached, from under the *rusary*. *Rusaries* themselves, in terms of material and color as well as techniques of wearing them, reveal a world of meaning. In upper-class neighborhoods of large cities, the designer labels of Gucci, Pierre Cardin, etc., are worn and sold openly. In sum, those who choose MR are always pushing the boundaries of the official dress code. It is this group that is labeled *malhijabi* and is the target of vigilante harassment and often denounced on the floor of the *Majles*. They are called lackeys of imperialism, whores, or antirevolutionary criminals who need to be educated or punished or both, depending on the political climate or the individual's perspective.

To the right are those who wear the *Hijab Islami* (HI) either because of their belief, job requirement, or political exigencies, signaling commitment to the Islamic Republic. This dress consists of the same *mantu* and *maghnae* of black material, either with pants or stockings, plus a *chador* that is tied around the head with bands. The shoes are heavy in winter and sandals in summer. The whole outfit is black. Those who don this attire are known as "Sisters." *Chador*, especially black *chador*, denotes a commitment to the regime among working women of the middle class. Being a traditional dress of Iranian women, not all *chadori* women are Sisters. *Chador* combined with *mantu* and *maghnae* is generally a good indicator of a woman's support for the regime. All women leaders interviewed wore HI.

The reasons for dress may vary from ideological commitment to occupational necessities or the husband's position and promotion. In one of our group discussions, a young woman with very modern attitudes toward gender roles wore *Hijab Islami*. Later, another member informed me that the young woman's husband is an aspiring under secretary in the cabinet, and she has to keep up an appearance in the public to help his job. I was reminded of corporate wives in American culture.

This dress code also allows variations, indicating status, fashion, and personal statement. The assistant to an under secretary to the minister of information was an attractive and well-groomed woman who wore an expensive *Hijab Islami*. While I waited in her office to meet the under secretary, she was carrying on a friendly conversation—too friendly by the Islamic Republic's standards—with a young man sitting next to her desk. She let her *chador*, which was not tied around her head, slip showing her designer *maghnae*. Her open and friendly manner was very different from the stern demure of the Sisters. She wore the dress code but did not follow the behavior code. She had *Hijab Islami*, but was not a Sister. Her relaxed behavior was more significant because it occurred in the office that is responsible for upholding and enforcing the Islamic ethic nationwide. Later, I met the minister himself, who was a modern, Western-educated clergyman of around forty. Indeed, the higher a person's position in the hierarchy, whether official or not, the more relaxed behavior they displayed. The zealots were often at lower levels of the administration.

None of these categories are absolute and cross-dressing occurs. However, it is mostly the MR crowd that has more freedom to wear HI than the Sisters. The other group has less freedom. Perhaps because they have more to lose should it be known that they have digressed from the Islamic ethic. In the summer of 1992, I learned that the editor of the leading women's magazine (*Zan-e-Rouz*) had left her post and started a liberal feminist magazine. She had also changed from HI to MR. To my informant, the latter was more important than the content of her magazine. She had switched camps and would not be forgiven by the Sisters.

In a group discussion, one informant jokingly said that she dresses for the occasion. When she goes to more conservative offices, such the Ministry of Justice, she will don HI to get the desired response, but if she is going to the Ministry of Foreign Affairs or Passport Office, she will wear MR and maybe some makeup.

This Islamic ethic also regulates men's behavior. Many men complained about restrictions on their behavior. Young men, in particular, face harassment from the morality squads. Short-sleeved, colorful shirts, jeans, foreign symbols, or logos on clothing, and punk haircuts are controlled. Smoking in office areas and laughing are disapproved of, too.

In the summer of 1989, I was researching the University of Tehran's regulations regarding women students. At this time, Islamic Societies dominated student affairs. A young man was assigned to meet and help me. He was about twenty years old, with the complete attire and expression of his group. He wore a black, long-sleeved, buttoned-up, loose shirt over his nondescript trousers. His face had a day-old stub. His hair was dark and cut short. His whole appearance expressed commitment to Islam and rejection of fashion and vanity. Had he been shaven and worn a smile, he would have shown a baby-faced young man. In addition to the prescribed stub beard, he wore a stern look on his face. He kept his hands at his side and kept a downcast eye. He also spoke very softly. Our conversation was frustrating. Since he would not look me in the face and mumbled under his lips, I had to bend to ask him questions and repeat myself. It must have been frustrating to him, too. Except for receiving a few pamphlets, I did not accomplish my goal there. The minister of information's open demeanor was a contrast to this young man's.

Hijab still remains central to the state's ideology and reflects shifts in power. A shift to the right is associated with denunciation of *malhijabi* from every public forum. For instance, after some relaxation of enforcement during the spring and summer of 1992 coinciding with the election and the opening of the new *Majles*, a coalition of the more conservative groups led to the denunciation of cultural invasion and *malhijabi*. In the winter of 1992–93, the conservatives, at least in terms of appearance, gained some momentum. One of my informants wrote that after closing counseling and guidance departments in high schools for thirteen years, they have now reopened them and asked those who were removed from their jobs to return. She, however, indirectly and later through her husband, was told that to maintain her new position she should wear *Hijab Islami*. Other female professionals have expressed the same pressure. The ongoing debate on the Islamic ethic leaves no doubt that the official line has abandoned returning women to the private domain of home and family. The complex network of the Islamic ethic draws an invisible though recognizable and enforceable line to mark the sex segregation. The woman's presence in the public domain is not marked just by her clothes, but also by her conduct. She faces restrictions in terms of behavior, speech, areas of activity, as well as social aspiration.

Women and Power

> I told these gentlemen: you always talk about Fatemeh (the Prophet's daughter)—example of Fatemeh—but only mention merits of her housekeeping and mothering activities and how obedient she was. You never mention her political activities . . . how she defended her husband and Islam. You only talk about her family roles [to women]. Why? Are you afraid that they [women] will get an upper hand? Do not fear them. Work together, side by side, and see how much you accomplish. (leader of the women's opposition group)

Several themes came through in interviews and group discussions about the relationship of women to power in the family and the society.

Woman as weaker sex. Regardless of their ideological stand, supporters and opponents of the Islamic Republic declared men and women equal and neither superior to the other. A member of an underground Marxist organization was surprised at my question: "Of course men and women are equal. You talk like a Western feminist." She continued, "Talking about men and women is designed to distract us from the main exploitation, the larger struggle, imperialist exploitation. . . . Women are brought to be submissive and are exploited." She, in another discussion, lamented the problems caused by women members who have no sense of group discipline. A director of a prep school and professor in a women's seminary, interviewed in 1989, stated:

> We must talk about humans and not men and women. . . . Social responsibility for women is different. Women can go to combat if necessary, take gun, there is no social responsibility that women cannot do, except judiciary and politics. Because she has a delicate spirit and is sensitive. . . . she is mother and is better for her not to be exposed to the criminals and corruption.

A theme repeated in the popular culture is that talking about men and women is divisive. "We are all humans and, in the Allah's eyes, gender is not a factor." My mother was among this group who saw my discussion of the sexes as "irrelevant." Nevertheless, she, like many others having said that, would list the real differences between men and women. The women's opposition leader stated: "Our *Shariat* has so many issues. As they [government] have initiated a reinterpretation [*Ijtehad*] of *Shariat* regarding the economic issues, the same should happen to women's issues; otherwise the exploitation will continue. Indeed, there should be no matriarchy, nor patriarchy; rather 'right-archy.' People's civic rights must be preserved. Division of labor at home must be based on justice." An administrative assistant at a company stated, "women are equal to men but have weaker minds. That is why we spend most of our time gossiping and chattering. Weaker minds."

Legal rights of the sexes, particularly in the family affairs, remained the focal point of many discussions. A director of a women's college, who was also a professor of a women's seminary and an unofficial advisor to the president in 1989, stated:

> Child custody is man's right. When a woman remarries she loses her independence. She becomes somebody's burden. As long as a woman has not married, she can take care of her children, but mother's husband can create moral problems. Men should not have unilateral divorce right. The true Islam is not actually implemented. In the true Islam we do not have divorce. Man must provide for woman and control his lust.

Interviewed again in 1992, she expressed more liberal views of women's rights.

Many leaders did not challenge the Islamic principles, rather they challenged their interpretation and implementation. Except for the Marxists, members of the legal opposition groups lauded Islamic provisions for women's rights and criticized the state's interpretation and implementation of them. It is imperative to mention that the existing opposition groups function within the framework of the state's ideology and do not challenge the primacy of Islam. The same leader of the opposition stated:

> They claim to be Muslims but are far from it. This regime has a political view of women, for political exploitation. Women suffer double exploitation. They have passed some laws, but their implementation is left to judges' discretion. . . . We still lack legal protection, but if men respect women's and children's rights, many of our problems will be solved.

During our two lengthy talks, she always sarcastically referred to the political leaders as "these gentlemen."

The debate about women's rights is a lively and ongoing debate. Five members of the original group were interviewed again in 1992. Three who had accepted man's unilateral right to divorce and child custody without any revision, now expressed a change of heart and proposed debate and change if necessary. The president's special advisor on woman's affairs stated, "Islam is dynamic, and not dead end. If something endangers Islamic community, then it is against Islam. We might have women judges in the next few (4) years."

The top woman. One of the interviewees holds the highest office occupied by a woman. There is no woman cabinet member yet, but she comes close to it. In 1991 a new position was added to the cabinet; a special council on women was created and the person in charge is a special adviser to the president on women's affairs. The first appointee is a thirty-eight-year-old woman, loyal to President Rafsanjani's faction. After two phone calls, I received an interview. Since she is the highest ranking woman, I have included most of her comments in this section.

I was to meet her at 10:00 A.M. in her special office in the presidential office complex in the central part of Tehran. Compared to 1989, the security check was more relaxed. At the main office, after I stated the purpose of my visit, the attendant asked for an identification card. I handed him my American driving licence. If he was surprised, it did not show. He filled out two forms and directed me to my destination through a maze of office buildings. I had to go to another building for a security check. This time the Sisters in charge were more pleasant. They also searched my handbag. One of them found a lipstick and a compact, which she removed from the bag. She told me to take them back when I returned. I could not understand the security significance of these items. They directed me to a new three-story building that is the Office of Women's Affairs. At the door, a sign warned men not to enter without prior notice.

The office had a homey atmosphere. Women wearing MRs behaved unencumbered and relaxed. The stern look of previous years or other offices was absent here. As far as *hijab* was concerned, they were all Sisters and their *hijab* must have been HI, consisting of a *mantu*, a *maghnae*, and a *chador*. In the office, they had removed their *chadors*—no man could come in without prior notice. The office had the feel and smell of a woman's environment—a private domain, a private public domain. I was reminded of typing pools in American offices.

The counsel, Mrs. Habibi, a robust young woman, with an open and friendly countenance, welcomed me to her office at 10:35. There was a young boy of about ten, her secretary's son, and a woman wearing MM—which I now knew to be of a fashionable kind—representative of the Jewish community in

Tehran. The two women had just returned from a trip to Germany and seemed to have a close rapport.

I had already learned that Mrs. Habibi has the president's support and is secure in her position. This came through in the three-hour-long discussion. The representative of the Jewish community remained in the office and participated in the discussion.

The goal of this office is to organize and orchestrate all issues and policies regarding women. Mrs. Habibi, like other leaders, offered the party line, which has changed since 1989. She advocated increased women's participation in public life. Her goals for a Muslim woman in the Islamic Republic were (a) to be an informed and educated mother; (b) to know her rights; (c) to pursue education; and (d) to actively participate in public life, including the labor market. She lauded women's efforts during the war period and indicated that women can now receive the Civil Medal of Honor. She considered illiteracy one of the major problems of women and blamed the previous regime and the imperialists (*Estekbar*) for this problem. She defined literacy as knowing one's rights and not just reading and writing. She acknowledged sex discrimination in hiring and mentioned efforts to remedy this situation. She added, "Since women are entitled to more vacation, the employers resist hiring them." She expressed a clear vision for empowering women by educating them about their rights in the family and the labor market. "We are here to get women what Islam has granted them. Our women need to take charge, I mean, stop being submissive. It is not Islamic."

Women leaders had a good general knowledge of *Shariat* and were pushing its interpretation. Among the new rights achieved is "marital pay" or alimony, which is new and was forwarded by women interpreting Islamic labor laws. The leaders revealed a sense of empowerment that was more due to their religious commitment than actual exercise of power.

Women professionals had a clear understanding of infringement of their power. One major impediment was restriction on their mobility. When their job required traveling in or outside of the city, they faced many restrictions. Most of these stemmed from procedural regulations and not specific laws. A hospital administrator complained that during the first year at her job, she had a difficult time getting her orders implemented by a staff of both men and women. Physicians objected to her checking on male patients. When she used the hospital vehicle to check on her suppliers, her higher-ups told her to use her own car. "They did not want a woman driving a hospital car." An agro-engineer was told not to use the department's jeep to travel, but rather to use her own car for office trips (*Zan-e-Rouz*, 1992:12).

Women traveling alone also face restrictions when checking into hotels. Until recently, a woman without male relatives was not allowed into hotels. The republic's paranoia about sexual corruption had led to banning women without male relatives from hotel rooms. It must be added that a single woman traveling—except in a few international chains—did not fare better before the revolution either. While the restrictions have been eased, hotel managers are still required to report a single woman guest to the police authorities.

A female lawyer complained that in arranging court dockets, female lawyers get the last priorities. The clerks, who are men, favor male lawyers and ignore the priority procedure. Furthermore, judges, who are mostly clergy now, sometimes show disdain for female lawyers which makes their work, especially in family cases, more difficult.

Woman's power in the family proved to be paramount for the participants at discussion groups. Child custody and divorce rights proved to be more pertinent than polygamy and mandatory *hijab*. The leaders took a more deliberate approach. They took pains to explain the Islamic underpinning of these rights. Some, despite my assurance of knowledge of the *Shariat*, explicated the rational and extreme circumstances proscribed for these rights.

The president of the state women's organization blamed men's lust and stated, "No matter how many laws we pass, we need to educate men to treat women right." The issues that seemed important to women were men's understanding and cooperation in household responsibilities, men's support of outside work or education, and disagreement about financial arrangement. Many complained that men appropriate their income and plan or spend it without their counsel. Women who worked often complained about their male colleagues and their husband's refusal to cooperate with them in their official tasks or household duties. A camera woman at National Iranian Television stated that sometimes she had to work at nights to cover the news. Her husband complained all the time and did not understand her occupational responsibilities.

For many middle-class women, a husband's infidelity has become a source of anxiety, too. This was new and not mentioned in the 1989 discussions. Indeed, the perception of promiscuity had increased so much that men and women who knew about my interest often approached me to inform and complain about moral decay and increased promiscuity.

Following a husband's infidelity, women fear divorce and losing their children. Divorce is dreaded for many reasons: losing one's status as a complete human being, which in many third world countries is obtained by being married; financial dependency; becoming a burden on relatives; and, foremost, losing custody of their children. Interestingly, polygamy and *hijab* were at the bottom of the list of women's concern.

Do women perceive that they are empowered by participating in the Islamic Revolution? The answer varies depending on specific issues, but I received more "No" responses than "Yes." The Islamic Republic is not to be solely blamed. Major social changes, such as the revolution, the war, economic shortages, constant social reorganization, rapid devaluation of one set of mores and harsh enforcement of another set, have all contributed to a sense of bewilderment and powerlessness.

Two points need further elaboration:

Men also share this sense of powerlessness. The economic factors are paramount in creating a sense of loss of control in individual affairs. Added to economic problems and exacerbating them are official experimentation with rules and regulations in all aspects of social life. The state, despite its major strides toward hegemony, still is fluid. What was legal yesterday may be illegal today.

Women are not passive victims of circumstances. The relationship between women and the Islamic Republic is dynamic and dialectical. Iranian women have shown amazing resilience in one of the major upheavals of the twentieth century. They have kept working, getting an education, and expanding the boundaries of their social lives. Contrary to the view of submissive Muslim women, they have resisted submission in an ingenious and continuous manner. Some women leaders were carrying a hectic schedule of managing large families and demanding jobs. Four among them had more than one job. These four were professors at a women's seminary in another town and traveled two days a week teaching there while having full-time jobs in Tehran.

Feminism

As a director of a women's college stated:

> There is an equilibrium in creation. What we see as inequality if we view it in its entirety is the soul of equality and justice. Woman with her unique psyche and physique, in different junctures [of her life], receives specific rights. Man, too, with his special physical and psychological features, receives specific rights under specific circumstances. None of this is due to inequality. . . . Woman is emotionally superior to man. This is a privilege and merit, and should not be defined as a fault. Woman has superior emotional quality and because of that has special responsibilities. God has done this in creating humans and achieving their perfection. . . . God has given women this responsibility, i.e., rearing of generation. . . . A great responsibility. She should undertake it and explain it to the world that having superior emotion is a valued quality and not an inferior one. A merit and a gift which woman has and having emotion does not mean lacking wisdom and judgement. One who has inferior judgement cannot have such a responsibility, cannot receive such a gift. Therefore, having more emotion does not mean having inferior mind.

Men and women are created differently but equally. Iranian women leaders do not spend time arguing that men and women are the same and should receive the same rights. They have accepted woman's nurturing capacity as her nature and proceed to maximize her rights within this framework. Their view of the sexes is very similar to the women of the New Christian Right, such as Phyllis Schlafly and others, who claim women are different and are entitled to different rights, protections, and responsibilities (Schlafly, 1981; see also Kaufman, 1994).

For women leaders in the Islamic Republic, the issue is the complementarity and compatibility of the sexes. Since each sex is created differently and with special responsibilities, women are entitled to financial security and the protection of men. In return, men ask for obedience. They do not see one as inferior to the other, thus they spend their time training women to be informed mothers and to pursue education.

For many middle-class girls, marriage and work go together. Marriage and motherhood are not choices, but rather givens. A director of an educational institution described a conversation she had with a student:

> Before you came, I was talking to this young lady, preparing her for her future roles, God willing, to become a valuable physician. . . . I was preparing her that in two years, when she takes the university's entrance exam, how difficult medical school is. I was informing her how much a woman who wants to be a physician must suffer. She cannot have a normal life. Why? Because it is necessary that you be a mother and form a family and do not let this natural part of your life be disturbed.

Starting from different potentials, leaders strive to reduce inequality in social opportunities. They emphasize education as the prime factor in improving women's opportunities. The Islamic Republic's constitution recognizes motherhood as woman's primary responsibility. Realizing the political underpinning of this premise, women leaders cloak their demands for women's rights in training future mothers to train the true Muslims. Whether they ask for sport facilities for girls, improved educational opportunities, television shows, legal rights, etc., they somehow wrap it in the flag of motherhood. For instance, in Islam, a woman's marital obligations are limited to sexual duty and residing in the husband's residence. The *Quran* does not require a woman to nurse her children. Therefore, a woman can ask for payment for nursing her children. Several women deputies have proposed legal provisions to be made in cases of divorce or parental abuse by adult children for women to receive compensation for nursing their children. The labor laws provide extended maternity leave, part-time employment (with full-time benefits), breaks for nursing mothers to nurse their children, on-site child care, etc. In this respect the Islamic Republic's regulations, not enforcements, resemble those of countries such as Sweden and Finland.

Having acknowledged woman's nurturing potential, women leaders, as well as others, move on to promote women's political activism as a must. A woman deputy, in a speech on women's week, after lauding the Islamic model of Fatemeh, calls on women to get involved in political affairs because this "is commended as one of their responsibilities" (*Etelat*, 1992:5). Compared to the last cabinet and *Majles*, the number of women deputies has doubled. The present *Majles* has nine female deputies. Two of them won on the first run of elections, compared to four men, in Iran's complicated parliamentary election system.

These all translate into an Islamic feminist consciousness that is different from secular feminist consciousness. If one must look for a Western example, European feminism comes to mind. As stated in chapter 3, this is "relational feminism," which seeks to establish women's rights in relation to her familial obligations. To begin with, the hegemony of the Islamic state has depended on women's indoctrination and resocialization. A concerted campaign of propaganda, purges, and intimidation reduced active resistance of the middle-class urban women. Almost a generation was either imprisoned, purged, or chose exile. Political oppression of women, unless they were accused of illegal political activities, is reduced. Some of those who were purged were invited back or changed occupation and returned to the labor market. Recently, those professional women abroad, who have not realized their potential, have debated returning home.

The propaganda has had two dimensions. One is to brand and condemn any behavior or value deemed harmful to the state's hegemony as antirevolutionary and exploitative, Western, or both. The second aspect promotes the state's agenda as

Islamic, true to woman's nature, and productive. Whenever women are the topic of an address or article, faults of the previous regime or Western societies are mentioned first, then Islam's rightful treatment of women and the Islamic Republic's achievements are commended. For example, a woman deputy, promoting a bill in the *Majles* to remove a ban on foreign travel of girls (young single women), first pointed out the exploitative treatment of women as sex objects in the West, then denounced restrictions on Iranian women realizing their true Islamic selves.

It is this two-pronged policy that has promoted a new feminist consciousness. To this end, to counteract the Mother's Day of the previous regime, the state first moved it to December 16, to coincide with Fatemeh's birthday. Then it was expanded to a week with festivities, celebrations, speeches, gifts, prizes, and honors for achieving women. In the same vein, though not centralized or orchestrated by the state, is the profusion of women's organizations. These groups, in competition with each other, organize seminars and conferences, publish materials, and promote a women's agenda. They range from ultraconservative to liberal moderate, which comes close to the state's approach. There are two organizations currently slightly to the left of the state. The left is underground and struggling. These organizations may serve an individual's political ends or may be tied to a political faction. Whatever their hidden or acknowledged agendas, they keep women's questions central to the regime's survival. They also result in increased women's consciousness. Such an overwhelming and unprecedented attention to women's issues is bound to generate a group consciousness. Another woman deputy states: "Shortcomings in women's affairs are due to administrative procedures not the legal provisions." She continued, "Women, by being informed about their rights, are their own best defenders." She then asks for women to organize nationwide (*Etelat*, 1992:7).

The minister of interior, a cleric, states, "Women should reject seclusion and participate in cultural and artistic gatherings to remove the current division in the society." In the same speech he declares, "a Muslim woman's insignia should not be a stern face, mourning, seclusion, and prying."

Solidarity. Organized efforts to increase women's consciousness has been basically a top-down process. Grass roots efforts are scattered and often short-lived. Middle-class women are adamant about improving their educational and occupational opportunities and their status in the family. They achieve these individually and with the help of their families rather than the organized assistance of other women. Bauer notes an increased cross-group cooperation among expatriated Iranian women in West Germany and increased consciousness of gender issues (Bauer, 1991). This heightened consciousness is partly the result of the host culture's impact on the immigrants. In Iran, women are the focal point of government discourse and a major theme of the state's propaganda. As a consequence, it has created an unprecedented consciousness of women's status—and as a corollary, gender roles.

Gender consciousness in the Iranian middle class implies women recognizing that they are a distinct social group with special problems, rights, and restrictions. However, like feminist consciousness everywhere, it is conditioned by class, ideology, ethnicity, and other social characteristics. One does not see the feminist solidarity of urban middle-class white American women in their counterparts in Iran. Among the leaders this comes through. Factional conflict affects women's organizations, too. A leader of a women's opposition group told me:

> One of our problems is lack of coordination between our women. I mean, women of our society with outlook, intelligence, and progressive ideas currently do not have cooperation. Due to the same mistakes going in the larger society. . . . I think there is a conspiracy against women. If they were united and cooperated, they could start a broad movement in the society which would make men, who control most of laws and rights, to follow.

I asked, "Do you believe men plot against women's uniting?" She responded, "It is possible, one suspects this. Men are not united either. Men, at least, are united about their issues, we women are not unified on our own issues either."

Those who are part of the establishment saw more unity and cooperation. "Before [the revolution] if eight or ten women were together, generally, they could not agree, but now you see that with a social trend, women from different walks of life are acting in unison and reacting accordingly. This is one feature of our revolution," stated a woman leader and member of the dominant political faction in 1989. Another stated, "Since the revolution, we have less jealousy and more unity. Attention to religious values has created more commitment, has reduced conflict and increased cooperation. Women are more committed then men, more motivated, more persistent and have more unity and togetherness than men."

The revolution has dichotomized women as far as their support for women's issues are concerned. Those who oppose the system, its Islamic orientation, and its treatment of women have found a shared concern. These women are not organized and center around professional, family, or community identity. They are mostly urban middle class women, some with professional training.

The supporters of the system and its ideology also have found reasons to cooperate and unify. During the early years of the revolution and the war period, they would participate in demonstrations or volunteer for the war efforts. Internal and external threats to the regime mobilized these women, not necessarily women's issues. Although they would demonstrate in denunciation of *malhijabi*. This group was more organized, either through the state's efforts or neighborhood committees managed and orchestrated by the community mosque. Members of this group came from the lower middle and working classes of urban areas.

Finally, one needs to mention the traditional support network of the extended family among women. Women of neighborhoods, tribes, family, or other collectivities are socialized to rely on each other in order to live. This type of mutual support is less conscious and more practical.

Since 1989, when the actual threat to the regime had diminished, women's attention, whether they were supporters or opponents of the system, has shifted to women's issues. Those who supported the system are very vocal to demand their rewards. The state through special programs does reward the veterans, their families, and has a special office for the families of the martyrs of the war.

The slight moderation of gender policies and sheer economic necessity have led some opponents of the system to return to Iran. They also ask for concessions in work regulations. Iranian media are rich with women of various orientations voicing their concerns. More than ever fundamentalist women and their liberal opposition are writing and publishing—one advocating motherhood as Allah's mandate and the other promoting Allah's demand for an educated and public woman. The women leaders sympathize with the former and live like the latter. Thus, they have created a symphony of praising Islam and asking for women's share of the Islamic pie.

Conclusion

The discourse of fundamentalism is fused with the issues of gender roles and modernism. As a resistance movement, it mobilizes the disenfranchised against internal and external enemies to realize a past moral system. Concerns about sexual morality lead fundamentalists to focus on gender roles in the family and the society. Modernism, or Westernism, is perceived to be responsible for this moral degeneration, which is personified as female. As such, fundamentalism is rife with female symbolism—negative, if sexual; positive, if maternal and submissive. Whether the veil, abortion, mother cow, *sati*, or any other example, gender dialogue reigns supreme in fundamentalist formulation. As Hawley states, "Women's behavior is regarded not only as being symptomatic of cosmic dislocation but as being its cause" (1994:27).

In the same vein is Riesebordt's idea that fundamentalism is "a protest against the assault on patriarchal structural principles in the family, economy and politics brought on by official policy, public disdain, and general moral erosion" (1993:202). Riesebordt's idea of "patriarchal structural principles" comes very close to our idea of gendered fundamentalism. We agree that fundamentalism is part of structural patriarchy and thus have no problem conceptualizing women fundamentalists, some of whom reach the higher echelons of its various organizations.

We disagree, however, with his notion of fundamentalism as anti-modern. Riesebordt contends that this "erosion of patriarchal norms and structures takes place primarily" in the private sphere (ibid.). He further points out that fundamentalism, like other movements, "readily employs the most modern technology and techniques" (ibid.:204). Here, again, this schizophrenic nature of fundamentalism becomes more comprehensible if we consider it as a gendered phenomenon: modern in the public domain and traditional in the private domain. Fundamentalists' obsession with high-tech machinery, particularly means of force (see Hawley, 1994:33) and their innovative organizational techniques, is far from traditional or anti-modern. The machismo of the leaders and their rhetorical references to power, militarism, and the romanticization of force is matched by their desire to dictate morality and control the family. Like many other social phenomena, fundamentalism displays contradictory features, combining traditional discourse on family with a modern orientation toward polity and economy.

Intolerance is often cited as a reason for fundamentalism's anti-modern nature. By the same token, many political orientations can be classified as such. Interestingly, Khomieni's Islamic Republic cooperated with, and later tolerated, Marxists in Iran for the first decade of the revolution but persecuted Islamic groups whom he considered to be revisionist. Christian America was defined as the Great Satan, while Iran expanded its relations with "godless" Marxists in the Soviet Union.

In an interesting turn of events, some NCR groups in America, in the spring of 1994, supported a woman who accused President Clinton of sexual harassment (*News-Leader*, 1994). The same groups were harsh in their criticism of Anita Hill, who accused Clarence Thomas of the same offense.

A gendered explanation of fundamentalism may not remedy its comparative complexities, but it can explicate some of the contradictory orientations of its organizations. For instance, the NCR, despite its claim to a pro-life and pro-family agenda, opposes the Family Leave Act (which allows employees to take unpaid leave to take care of family emergencies) and gun control, as well as tax benefits for child care or any social assistance program. This may seem irrational and inconsistent until one considers the gendered nature of fundamentalism, which renders these seeming inconsistencies more congruent. In a Senate hearing, Ms. Schlafly opposed child care and the Family Leave Act, claiming that they benefit two-career yuppie couples (quoted in Marshall, 1991:58). Any privilege or benefit accorded to dual career couples or poor women is perceived to attack the notion of the homemaker wife. If women stayed home and men took their financial responsibilities seriously, there would be no need for the Family Leave Act.

The "ideal of womanhood," as Papanek suggests, is used as a tool to extract conformity and maintain boundaries (1994; see also Hawley, 1994). Therefore, groups or governments that are concerned with preserving the family are malleable toward militarism. With regard to gun control, for instance, the NCR sees that as a limitation on men's behavior, while abortion or the Equal Rights Amendment would unleash female selfishness, promote promiscuity, and eventually destroy the hierarchical family. Furthermore, the gun is a masculine symbol. Male sexuality requires female modesty just as militarism points to the victim's responsibility. One is tempted to look for a correlation of sex and violence in fundamentalist discourse. Aid to Families with Dependent Children, the Family Leave Act, and the Women, Infants and Children Program benefit either working or poor women for whom fundamentalist women have little sympathy. The state helping women instead of their men taking care of them disrupts traditional family.

Harris rejects the usefulness of the term "fundamentalism" altogether and proposes that the fundamentalists' supposed need to control women is feminists' projection of their own orientation toward fundamentalism. "I know of no evidence indicating that Jewish women living within the 'fundamentalist' orbit have, as a group, been special targets of the anger and hatred that are hypothesized to be directed against the 'other'" (1994:164).

The issue of women's rights within the fundamentalist discourse has two dimensions: lost rights and lost opportunities for rights. The first one is easy to quantify by jobs lost, opportunities denied, education restricted, laws abolished or created to constrict women's rights. The second one, while still unquantifiable, requires some imagination or even conjecture. Had the Equal Rights Amendment passed, women would not have had to wait until 1994 to have a federally guaranteed right to unpaid maternity leave. The issue of job segregation would have been more easily rectified than through litigation. As I have mentioned elsewhere (see Gerami, 1989), part of fundamentalism's damage to women is in opportunities lost for improving women's life chances, or in hopes lost for their daughters.

Fundamentalists' notion of the ideal society is inseparably linked to the notion of the ideal woman. This research was postulated to gauge women's support for this "ideal" in three countries marked by viable and thriving fundamentalist movements, though socioeconomically different. Moghadam (1994) criticizes the idea of culture as an independent variable. Due to the same complexities and to avoid reductionism, I refrained from conceptualizing fundamentalism as an independent variable affecting women's self-identity. Rather, I decided to measure women's support for "the ideal woman" who dwells in her own sphere, performs her natural feminine functions, leaves power and politics to men—unless perhaps in her own hemisphere—and rejects the "fanciful" ideals of feminism in terms of gender equality. Four indexes measured these aspects cross-culturally.

In Egypt and Iran, not surprisingly, women's identity is inseparably linked to motherhood. Numerous encounters with Iranian and other Middle Eastern women have convinced me that the majority have internalized motherhood as the *core* of their personhood. Other *options* radiate from this core. I would like to reiterate that motherhood is rarely seen as an option, while other activities are optional. The survey results also revealed that motherhood, for Egyptian and Iranian women, is the essence of their self-identity.

Women in Iran and Egypt are solidly grounded in the family. This self-identity, it must be pointed out, precedes fundamentalism and is inherent in Muslim Middle Eastern cultures. Fundamentalist movements have reaffirmed this orientation. Had secularization continued, as in Turkey, women's familial identity would have been weakened. Fundamentalists have been successful in that regard.

Starting with the familial roles, the Muslim women samples rejected spatial segregation as desired by fundamentalists. They then proceeded to claim an inalienable right to the public domain, its market and its politics. Interestingly, fundamentalists' concern about morality and sexuality has created new opportunities for women. In Iran and Egypt, increasing numbers of women enter various health care fields to reduce women's need for male health care providers.

An open-ended question asked the Egyptian sample to name their favorite role model. The first category with highest frequency was their mothers. The second category was female political leaders, such as Mrs. Bhutto and Mrs. Aquino. Finally, religious personalities, like the prophet's wives, were mentioned with less than 20 percent frequency.

For American women, the issue is less clear. The changes caused by the women's movement have challenged the relational identity of woman as mother and homemaker, but have not completely removed family as the defining factor in women's identity. Fundamentalists' call to validate motherhood as a socially credible *choice* resonated in this study. Coming a full circle, the NCR has propelled motherhood to be considered as a woman's deliberate decision in her life course rather than a biological *given*. With baby boomers opting for late pregnancies, the idea of combining "relational" and "individualistic" identity is most desirable. Indeed, the NCR has been successful in bringing family to the forefront of the public discourse.

In the preceding chapters, I discussed lost opportunities due to the rise of fundamentalism in the three countries. Observers have enumerated fundamentalism's adverse effects on women's rights and life chances around the world. With varying degrees of intensity, the effects can be summarized broadly as

- reaffirming motherhood as the core of woman's identity;
- reaffirming family as woman's sui generis domain;
- constructing family as a tool of political manipulation and conformity;
- constructing female symbolism as a vehicle of boundary maintenance;
- fetishizing female sexuality as destructive; and, as a result
- reifying the ideal woman as a dehumanized, submissive, asexual, and selfless being.

This research, as well as other works, has delineated the specific social and political measures emanating from these premises. The constrictive measures vary depending on the socioeconomic texture of a given society and women's ethnic or social class.

Now I want to do the unthinkable and look for the bright side of fundamentalism. This is easier to formulate in the case of Muslim Middle Eastern countries. To begin with, these movements have

- politicized lower urban middle and working class women who had not been mobilized, as such, in independence or bourgeois movements in Iran, Egypt, or Pakistan;

- propelled a large number of women, for the first time, to learn the sacred texts and men's way of interpreting them; it may be hoped that this quantitative participation will lead to a qualitative shift in a female-friendly interpretation of the sacred texts;

- created a grass roots cadre of movement carriers to broaden the scope of a women's movement beyond the upper middle class, should it materialize in future; and

- as a result of the above factors, fostered the groundwork for an indigenous women's movement rather than a duplication of Western ways of pursuing women's rights.

With regard to American women, the backlash stirred by the fundamentalist discourse

- is carried mostly by lower middle class women who checked the eccentricities of the women's movement generated by some of its carriers;

- has broadened the movement's spectrum to include larger constituencies who may not be carriers but sympathizers; and

- has reaffirmed motherhood as a legitimate feminist agenda.

Comparing fundamentalism in these countries reveals an interesting insight with regard to the ideal of motherhood. Whereas in the United States, the NCR has managed to recast motherhood as a *choice*, Islamic fundamentalists are pursuing it as a *given*. Among other factors, this striking difference is due to the maturity of women's movements in the two camps. American feminists promoted an individualistic identity distinct from woman's familial roles. The fundamentalists' discourse is recasting motherhood as a choice in the feminist canon. This might have been an unintended, and for some even an undesirable, formulation of their gender ideology. Kaufman (1994) draws an interesting comparison between fundamentalist Jewish women and radical feminists, who, though starting from different perspectives, call for celebration of woman's unique physical and cultural features.

Islamic fundamentalists, on the other hand, nipping a very young feminist movement in the bud and under the banner of nature's mandate, pushed women further into the family. They managed to cast woman's individualistic identity as a perversion of her nature plotted by Western imperialists. Lately, I can hear weak dissenting voices of Islamic feminists formulating motherhood as a choice requiring a woman's deliberate consideration (*Zan-e-Rouz*, various issues). Generally, however, as far as fundamentalists are concerned, motherhood is womanhood, whether by nature or nurture.

In the United States, the NCR women forward a discourse of feminine rights that is similar to Islamic feminists' agenda. Both oppose gender equality for gender complementarity, advocate protective rights for women, and acknowledge man's role as provider and protector. Both groups come from the lower middle classes, with limited college education, and may be a first-generation urban resident.

In summary, fundamentalists' ideal of a protected and private family, with woman as the functionary and man as the gatekeeper, has attracted only a minority in the three countries studied here. This, though, is a substantial minority and very vocal in all three societies. The movements, nevertheless, have shifted the sociopolitical landscape for all women. Feminists have an obligation to listen to these voices and, if genuine, to consider their choices.

Bibliography

Abbott, Pamela and Claire Wallace. 1992. *The Family and the New Right*, London: Pluto Press.

Abdel Kader, Soha. 1987. *Egyptian Women in a Changing Society, 1899–1987*, Boulder, CO: Lynne Rienner Publishers.

Abu-Laughod, Lila. 1986. *Veiled Sentiments: Honor and Poetry in a Bedouin Society*, Berkeley: University of California Press.

Adams, Carolyn and Kathryn Winston. 1980. *Mothers at Work*, New York: Longman.

Ahmed, Leila. 1992. *Women and Gender in Islam: Historical Roots of a Modern Debate*, New Haven, CT: Yale University Press.

Al-Ahmad, Jalal. 1977. *Gharbzadegi* (Westoxication), Tehran: New Books.

al-Ghazzali. 1909. *The Confessions of al=Ghazzali*. Trans. Cloud Field. London: Gidden.

Altorki, S. 1986. *Women in Saudi Arabia*, New York: Columbia University Press.

Amin, G. 1981. "Some Economic and Cultural Aspects of Economic Liberalization in Egypt," *Social Problems*, 28(4):430–441.

Ardener, Edwin. 1972. "Belief and the Problem of Women," in Jean LaFontaine (Ed.), *The Interpretation of Ritual: Essays in Honor of A.I. Richards*, London: Tavistock.

Asad, Talal. 1970. *The Kababish Arabs: Power, Authority and Consent in a Nomadic Tribe*, London: C. Hurst.

Ashraf, A. and M. Sedighi. 1978. "The Role of Women in Iranian Development," in Aspen Institute of Humanistic Studies. *Iran: Past, Present, and Future*, 201–312.

Aswad, Barbara. 1967. "Key and Peripheral Roles of Noble Women in a Middle East Plains Village," *Anthropological Quarterly* 40(3):139–153.

————. 1978. "Women, Class, and Power: Examples from Hatay, Turkey," in Beck and Keddie (Eds.), *Women in the Muslim World*, Cambridge, MA: Harvard University Press.

Ayubi Nazih, M. 1980. "The Political Revival of Islam: The Case of Egypt," *International Journal of the Middle East* 12:481–499.

Azari, F. 1983. "The Post-Revolutionary Women's Movement in Iran," in Azari, F. (Ed.), *Women of Iran*, London: Ithaca Press.

Aziza, Hussein. 1985. "Recent Amendment to Egypt's Personal Status Law," in E.W. Fernea (Ed.), *Women and the Family in the Middle East: New Voices of Change*, 231–232, Austin: University of Texas Press.

Badran, Margot. 1989. "The Origins of Feminism in Egypt," in A. Angerman et al. (Eds.), *Current Issues in Women's History*, 153–170, London: Routledge.

————. 1994. "Gender Activism: Feminists and Islamists in Egypt," in Valentine Moghadam (Ed.), *Identity Politics and Women*, 202–228. Boulder, CO: Westview Press.

Bahry, L. 1982. "The New Saudi Woman: Modernizing in an Islamic Framework," *Middle East Journal* 36(4):502–515.

Bainton, Roland. 1957. *What Christianity Says About Sex, Love, and Marriage*, New York: Association Press.

Barnett, Sharon and Richard Harris. 1982. "Recent Changes in Predictors of Abortion Attitudes," *Sociology and Social Research* 66:320–334.

Barr, James. 1981. *Fundamentalism*, London: SCM Press.

Basow, Susan. 1992. *Gender: Stereotypes and Roles*, Pacific Grove, CA: Brooks/Cole.

Bauer, Janet. 1983. "Poor Women and Social Consciousness in Revolutionary Iran," in Nashat (Ed.), *Women and Revolution in Iran*, Boulder, CO: Westview Press.

————. 1991. "A Long Way Home: Islam in the Adaptation of Iranian Women Refugees in Turkey and West Germany," in Asghar Fathi (Ed.), *Iranian Refugees and Exile Since Khomeini*, 77–101, Costa Mesa, CA: Mazda.

Beck, L. and N. Keddie (Eds.). 1978. *Women in the Muslim World*, Cambridge, MA: Harvard University Press.

Beck, Roy. 1992. "Washington's Profamily Activists," *Christianity Today* (November 9): 21–26.

Bernard, C. 1980. "Islam and Women: Some Reflections on the Experience of Iran," *Journal of South Asian and Middle Eastern Studies* 4:10–26.

Bernard, Jessie. 1981. *The Female World*, New York: Free Press.

Betteridge, A. 1983. "To Veil or Not to Veil: A Matter of Protest or Policy," in Nashat (Ed.), *Women and Revolution in Iran*, 109–129, Boulder, CO: Westview Press.

Blake, Judith. 1980. "Abortion and Public Opinion: The 1960–1970 Decade," *Science* 71:540–549.

Boles, Janet. 1979. *The Politics of the Equal Rights Amendment: Conflict and the Decision Process*, New York: Longman.

Bradley, Karen and Diana Khor. 1993. "Toward an Integration of Theory and Research on the Status of Women,"*Gender and Society* 7(3) (September): 347–379.

Bromley, David and Anson Shupe (Eds.). 1984. *New Christian Politics*, Macon, GA: Mercer University Press.

Bruce, Steve. 1987. "The Moral Majority: The Politics of Fundamentalism in Secular Society," in Caplan, Lionel (Ed.), *Studies in Religious Fundamentalism*, 177–194, New York: State University of New York Press.

———. 1992. "Revelations: The Future of the New Christian Right," in Lawrence Kaplan (Ed.), *Fundamentalism in Comparative Perspective*, 38–73, Amherst: University of Massachusetts Press.

Bullough, Vern. 1973. *The Subordinate Sex: A History of Attitudes Toward Women*, Urbana: University of Illinois Press.

Campo, Juane. 1991. *The Other Side of Paradise: Explorations into the Religious Meaning of Domestic Space in Islam*, Columbia: University of South Carolina.

Caplan, Lionel (Ed.). 1987. *Studies in Religious Fundamentalism*, New York: State University of New York Press.

Census Bureau. 1987. *Census of Iranian Population*, Tehran: Census Bureau.

Chafe, William H. 1977. *Women and Equality: Changing Patterns in American Culture*, New York: Oxford University Press.

Chalafant, Paul, Robert Beckley, and Eddie Palmer. 1987. *Religion in Contemporary Society*, Palo Alto, CA: Mayfield.

Chandler, Ralph. 1984. "The Fundamentalist Heritage of the New Christian Right," in David Bromley and Anson Shupe (Eds.), *New Christian Politics*, 41–61, Macon, GA: Mercer University Press.

Chase-Dunn, Christopher. 1975. "The Effects of International Economic Dependence on Development and Inequality: A Cross-National Study," *American Sociological Review* 40:720–738.

———. 1983. "Inequality, Structural Mobility, and Dependency Reversal in Capitalist World-Economy," in Doran et al. (Eds.), *North/South Relations: Studies of Dependency Reversal*, 73–95, New York: Praeger.

Conover, Pamela Johnston and Virginia Gray. 1983. *Feminism and the New Right: Conflict over American Family*, New York: Praeger.

Crapanzano, Vincent. 1972. "The Hamadsha," in Nikki Keddie (Ed.), *Scholars, Saints and Sufis: Muslim Religious Institutions Since 1500*, 327–348, Berkeley: University of California Press.

Douglas, M. 1970. *Natural Symbols: Explorations in Cosmology*, New York: Random House.

Doumato, Elenor. 1991. "Hearing Other Voices: Christian Women and the Coming of Islam," *International Journal of the Middle East Studies* 23(2):177–199.

Dos Santos, T. 1970. "The Structure of Dependence," *American Economic Review* 40:231–236.

Durham, Martin. 1985. "Family, Morality and the New Right," *Parliamentary-Affairs* 38(2):180–191.

Dworkin, Andrea. 1982. *Right-wing Women*, New York: Coward-McCann.

Ehrenreich, Barbara. 1983. *The Hearts of Men: American Dreams and the Flight from Commitment*, New York: Anchor.

El Guindi, F. 1981. "Veiling Infitah with Muslim Ethic: Egypt's Contemporary Islamic Movement," *Social Problems* 28(4):465–485.

Elliot, Elisabeth. 1976. *Let Me Be a Woman*, Wheaton, IL: Tyndale House.

Ellman, Mary. 1968. *Thinking About Women*, New York: Harcourt.

Elshtain, Jean Bethke. 1981. *Public Man, Private Woman: Women in Social and Political Thought*, Princeton, NJ: Princeton University Press.

Epstein, C.F. 1988. *Deceptive Distinctions: Sex, Gender and the Social Order*, New Haven, CT: Yale University Press.

Esposito, John L. 1982. *Women in Muslim Family Law*, Syracuse, NY: Syracuse University Press.

———. 1992. *The Islamic Threat: Myth or Reality?* New York: Oxford University Press.

Etelat. Saturday 14-12-92 (24-9-1371):5.

———. Thursday, 9-12-92 (19-9-1371):7.

Evans, P. 1979. *Dependent Development,* Princeton, NJ: Princeton University Press.

Exter, Thomas and Frederick Barber. 1986. "The Age of Conservatism," *American Demographics* (November):30–37.

Falwell, Jerry. 1980. *Listen America!,* Garden City, NY: Doubleday.

Fanon, Frantz. 1965. *A Dying Colonialism,* New York: Grove Press.

Farrag, Amina. 1971. "Social Control amongst the Mzabite Women of Beni-Isguen," *Middle Eastern Studies* Winter (3):317–327.

Ferdows, Adele. 1983. "Women and the Islamic Revolution in Iran," *International Journal of the Middle East Studies* 15:283–298.

Fischer, M. 1978. "On Changing the Concept and Position of Persian Women," in Beck and Keddie (Eds.), *Women in the Muslim World,* 189–216, Cambridge, MA: Harvard University Press.

Freeman, Jo. 1975. *The Politics of Women's Liberation,* New York: David McKay.

Friedl, E. 1975. *Women and Men: An Anthropologist's View,* New York: Holt, Rinehart & Winston.

———. 1989. *Women of Deh Koh,* Washington, DC: Smithsonian Institution Press.

Gerami, Shahin. 1988. "Women's Public Power in Muslim and Catholic Countries," unpublished, presented at the meetings of the Society for Study of Social Problems, Atlanta.

———. 1989a. "Privatization of Women's Role in the Islamic Republic of Iran," in Benavides and Daley (Eds.), *Religion and Political Power,* Albany: State University of New York Press.

———. 1989b. "Questionnaire," *Zan-e-Rouz,* 25 July, No. 1223 (17-4-1368):insert.

———. 1989c. "Religious Fundamentalism as a Response to Foreign Dependency: The Case of the Iranian Revolution," *Social Compass* 36(4):451–467.

———. 1993. "Woman's Body and Her Identity in Iranian Culture," *Kankash* (12):75–93.

Gerson, Kathleen. 1985. *Hard Choices: How Women Decide About Work, Career, and Motherhood,* Berkeley: University of California Press.

Gilder, George. 1974. *Naked Nomads: Unmarried Men in America,* New York: Quadrangle/New York Times Book.

———. 1981. *Wealth and Poverty,* New York: Basic Books.

Hadden, Jeffrey and Anson Shupe (Eds.). 1986. *Prophetic Religions and Politics*, New York: Paragon House.

———. (Eds.). 1989. *Secularization and Fundamentalism Reconsidered*, New York: Paragon House.

Haeri, Shahla. 1980. "Women, Law and Social Change in Iran," in Smith, J. (Ed.), *Women in Contemporary Muslim Societies*, 209–325, London: Bucknell University Press.

Hargrove, Barbara, Jean Schmidt, and Sheila Davaney. 1985. "Religion and the Changing Role of Women," *Annals, AAPSS* 480 (July): 117–131.

Harris, Jay. 1994. "Fundamentalism: Objection from a Modern Jewish Historian," in J.S. Hawley (Ed.), *Fundamentalism and Gender*, 137–175, Oxford: Oxford University Press.

Hartmann, David. 1988. *The Springfield Survey of Local Needs* (Summer), Springfield, MO: Center for Social Research.

Hassan, R. 1987. "Equal before Allah?: Woman-Man Equality in the Islamic Tradition," *Harvard Divinity Bulletin* 2:2–7.

Hawley, John S. 1994. *Fundamentalism and Gender*, Oxford: Oxford University Press.

Heberlein, T. and R. Baumgartner. 1978. "Factors Affecting Response Rates to Mailed Questionnaires: A Quantitative Analysis of the Published Literature," *American Sociological Review* 43 (August): 447–462.

Hegland, Mary. 1983. "Aliabad Women: Revolution as Religious Activity," in G. Nashat (Ed.), *Women and the Revolution in Iran*, 171–195, Boulder, CO: Westview Press.

Heinz, Donald. 1983. "The Struggle to Define America," in Robert Libman and Robert Wuthnow (Eds.), *The New Christian Right: Mobilization and Legitimation*, 133–146, New York: Aldine Publishing Company.

Henning, C. 1974. "Canon Law and the Battle of the Sexes," in Ruether (Ed.), *Religion and Sexism*, New York: Simon and Schuster.

Higgin, Patricia. 1985. "Women in the Islamic Republic of Iran: Legal, Social, and Ideological Changes," *Signs* (Spring) 10(31):477–494.

Hijab, N. 1988. *Womanpower: The Arab Debate on Women at Work*, Cambridge, MA: Cambridge University Press.

Hoffman-Ladd, Valerie. 1987. "Polemics on the Modesty and Segregation of Women in Contemporary Egypt," *International Journal of the Middle East* 19:23–50.

Hossain, R. 1988. *Sultana's Dream*, New York: Feminist Press.

Ibrahim, Y.M. 1979. "Iran's New Women Rebel at Returning to the Veil," *New York Times*, March 11, IV 2:3.

————. 1983. "Inside Iran's Cultural Revolution," *New York Times*, April 18: No. 2.

International Institute for Adult Literacy. "Woman's Place," Tehran, Undated.

Jalal, Ayesha. 1991. "The Convenience of Subservience: Women and the State of Pakistan," in Deniz Kandiyoti (Ed.), *Women, Islam and State*, 77–113. Philadelphia, PA: Temple University Press.

Jayawardena, Kumari. 1986. *Feminism and Nationalism in the Third World*, London: Zed Books.

Kagitcibasi, C. 1986. "Status of Women in Turkey: Cross-Cultural Perspective," *International Journal of Middle East Studies* 18:485–499.

Kaplan, Lawrence (Ed.). 1992. *Fundamentalism in Comparative Perspective*, Amherst: University of Massachusetts Press.

Kaufman, Debra R. 1994. "Paradoxical Politics: Gender Politics among Newly Orthodox Jewish Women in the United States," in Valentine Moghadam (Ed.), *Identity Politics and Women*, 349–367. Boulder, CO: Westview Press.

Kayhan Havai. "Can You be a Role Model for Women?" March 1988, No. 820 (1-1-1368):6–7.

Keddie, Nikki. 1979. "Problems in the Study of the Middle Eastern Women," *International Journal of the Middle Eastern Studies* 10 (May):225–40.

————. 1983. *An Islamic Response to Imperialism*, Berkeley: University of California Press.

Khaamenie, Ayatollah. "I Support All Women Becoming Scientists in All Areas," *Zan-e-Rouz*, Saturday 12-20-92, No. 1389 and 1390, (21-9-1371):7 and 86.

Khalidi, Ramala and Judith Tucker. 1992. *Women's Rights in the Arab World*, Washington: MERIP.

Klatch, Rebecca. 1987. *Women of the New Right*, Philadelphia, PA: Temple University Press.

————. 1988. "Coalition and Conflict among Women of the New Right," *Signs* 4:671–694.

Lawrence, Bruce. 1989. *Defenders of God*, San Francisco, CA: Harper and Row.

Lévi-Strauss, C. 1956. "The Family," in H. Shapiro (Ed.), *Man, Culture, and Society*, New York: Oxford University Press.

Libman, Robert C. and Robert Wuthnow (Eds.). 1983. *The New Christian Right: Mobilization and Legitimation*, New York: Aldine.

Lienhardt, Peter. 1972. "Some Social Aspects of the Trucial States," in D. Hopwood (Ed.), *The Arabian Peninsula: Society and Politics*, 219–229, London: Allen and Unwin.

Lipset, S. and E. Raab. 1970. *The Politics of Unreason: Right-Wing Extremism in America, 1790–1970*, New York: Harper and Row.

Mahowald, Mary Briody (Ed.). 1983. *Philosophy of Woman: An Anthology of Classical and Current Concepts*, Indianapolis, IN: Hackett.

Mansbridge, Jane J. 1986. *Why We Lost the ERA*, Chicago, IL: University of Chicago Press.

Marsden, George. 1980. *Fundamentalism and American Culture*, New York: Oxford University Press.

Marshall, Susan. 1984. "Paradoxes of Change: Culture Crisis, Islamic Revival, and the Reactivation of Patriarchy," *Journal of Asian and African Studies* 19(1–2):1–17.

———. 1991. "Who Speaks for American Women? The Future of Antifeminism," *ANNALS AAPSS* 515 (May):50–62.

Marshall, Susan and Jeffrey Stokes. 1981. "Tradition and the Veil: Female Status in Tunisia and Algeria," *Journal of Modern African Studies* 19:4.

Marsot, A.L. 1977. *Egypt's Liberal Experiment: 1922–1936*, Los Angeles: University of California Press.

Marty, Martin. 1992. "Fundamentals of Fundamentalism," in Lawrence Kaplan (Ed.), *Fundamentalism in Comparative Perspective*, 15–23, Amherst: University of Massachusetts Press.

McCarthy Brown, Karen. 1994. "Fundamentalism and the Control of Women," in John S. Hawley (Ed.), *Fundamentalism and Gender*, 175–203, Oxford: Oxford University Press.

Mead, Margaret. 1963. *Sex and Temperament in Three Primitive Societies*, New York: Morrow.

Mernissi, Fatima. 1987. *Beyond the Veil*, Bloomington and Indianapolis: Indiana University Press.

Minai, N. 1981. *Women in Islam, Tradition and Transition in the Middle East*, New York: Seaview Book.

Moghadam, Valentine. 1988. "Women, Work, and Ideology in the Islamic Republic," *International Journal of Middle East Studies* 2:221–243.

——. 1992. "Fundamentalism and the Woman Question in Afghanistan," in Lawrence Kaplan (Ed.), *Fundamentalism in Comparative Perspective*, 126–151, Amherst: University of Massachusetts Press.

——. 1993. *Modernizing Women: Gender and Social Change in the Middle East*, Boulder, CO: Lynne Rienner.

——. 1994. *Identity Politics and Women*, Boulder, CO: Westview Press.

Mottahari, Murtiza. 1974 (1359). *Nizam-i Huguqi zan dar Islam* (Women's Right in Islam), Tehran: Islamic Press.

Mumtaz, Khawar. 1994. "Identity Politics and Women: 'Fundamentalism' and Women in Pakistan," in Valentine Moghadam (Ed.), *Identity Politics and Women*, 228–242, Boulder, CO: Westview Press.

Murdock, George. 1937. "Comparative Data on the Division of Labor by Sex," *Social Forces* 15:553.

——. 1949. *Social Structure*, New York: Macmillan.

Murray, Jessica. 1972. "Male Perspective in Language," *Women: A Journal of Liberation* 3:46–50.

Najmabadi, Afsaneh. 1991. "Hazards of Modernity and Morality: Women, State and Ideology in Contemporary Iran," in Deniz Kandiyoti (Ed.), *Women, Islam and State*, 48–76, Philadelphia, PA: Temple University Press.

Nashat, G. 1980. "Women in the Islamic Republic of Iran," *Iranian Studies* 13(1–4):165–94.

——. (Ed.). 1983. *Women and Revolution in Iran*, Boulder, CO: Westview Press.

Nelson, Cynthia. 1974. "Public and Private Politics: Women in the Middle Eastern World," *American Ethnologist* 1(3):551–565.

News-Leader. 1994. "Religious Right Uses Latest Charges to Weaken Clinton," May 15:8A.

Newsweek. 1992. "Schlafly's Son: Out of the GOP Closet," September 28:18.

NORC. 1988. *General Social Survey*, Chicago, IL: NORC.

Nuri, Yahya. 1961 (1340). *Haugh va Hughug-e Zan dar Islam* (Rights and Responsibilities of Women in Islam), Tehran: n.p.

O'Brien, Denise. 1977. "Female Husbands in Southern Bantu Societies," in Alice Schlegel (Ed.), *Sexual Stratification*, 109–126, New York: Columbia University Press.

Offen, Karen. 1988. "Defining Feminism: A Comparative Historical Approach," *Signs* 14(1):119–157.

Ortner, Sherry. 1974. "Is Female to Male as Nature is to Culture?" in Michelle Rosaldo and Louise Lamphere (Eds.), *Woman, Culture, and Society*, 67–88, Stanford, CA: Stanford University Press.

Paige, Connie. 1987. "Watch on the Right," *Ms.*, February: 24–28.

Papanek, Hanna. 1985. "Class and Gender in Education-Employment Linkages," *Comparative Education Review* 29(3):14–25.

———. 1994. "The Ideal Woman and the Ideal Society: Control and Autonomy in the Construction of Identity," in Valentine Moghadam (Ed.), *Identity Politics and Women*, 42–76, Boulder, CO: Westview Press.

Parsons, T., and R.F. Bales. 1955. *Family, Socialization, and Interaction Process*, Glencoe, IL: Free Press.

Phillip, Thomas. 1978. "Feminism and Nationalist Politics in Egypt," in Beck and Keddie (Eds.), *Women in the Muslim World*, 277–295, Cambridge: Harvard University Press.

Pollack Petchesky, Rosalind. 1981. "Antiabortion, Antifeminism, and the Rise of the New Right," *Feminist Studies* 7 (Summer):206–246.

Prediss (a Persian newspaper). 1981. No. 14, March 21 (1-1-1360):1.

Rafsanjani, H. 1990a. "Tehran Tries Weaving Both Chador Cloth, Chador Rules," *Iran Times*, December 28, Vol. 20, No. 43:16.

———. 1990b. "Those Who Enjoy Good Life Can Have a Harem," *Iran Times*, August 3, Vol. 20, No. 22:5.

Rahnavard, Zahra. 1990. "Harassments about Hijab," *Iran Times*, June 8, Vol. 20, No. 11:1.

Ramazani, N. 1985. "Arab Women in the Gulf," *Middle East Journal* 2:258–276.

Rapp, Rayna. 1979. "Anthropology," *Signs* 4(3):497–513.

Riesebordt, Martin. 1993. *Pious Passion: The Emergence of Modern Fundamentalism in the United States and Iran*, Los Angeles: University of California Press.

Rogers, Susan Carol. 1978. "Woman's Place: A Critical Review of Anthropological Theory," *Comparative Studies in Society and History* 20(1):123–173.

Rosaldo, Michelle Z. 1974. "Women, Culture, and Society: A Theoretical Overview, " in Michelle Z. Rosaldo and Louise Lamphere (Eds.), *Women, Culture, and Society*, Stanford, CA: Stanford University Press.

Rosaldo, Michelle Z. and Louise Lamphere (Eds.). 1974. *Woman, Culture, and Society*, Stanford, CA: Stanford University Press.

Rubenstein, Richard. 1986. "God and Caesar in Conflict in the American Polity," in Jeffrey Hadden and Anson Shupe (Eds.), *Secularization and Fundamentalism Reconsidered*, 201–214, New York: Paragon House.

Ruether, R. (Ed.). 1974. *Religion and Sexism*, New York: Simon & Schuster.

Ryan, M.P. 1983. *Womanhood in America: From Colonial Times to the Present*, New York: Franklin Watts.

Sabbah, Fatna. 1984. *Woman in the Muslim Unconscious*, New York: Pergamon Press.

Saiedi, Nader. 1986. "What is Islamic Fundamentalism?" in Jeffrey Hadden and Anson Shupe (Eds.), *Prophetic Religions and Politics*, 173–195, New York: Paragon House.

Sandeen, Ernest. 1970. *The Roots of Fundamentalism*, Chicago, IL: University of Chicago Press.

Sansarian, E. 1982. *The Women's Rights Movement in Iran: Mutiny, Appeasement, and Repression from 1900 to Khomeini*, New York: Praeger.

Sayigh, R. 1981. "Roles and Functions of Arab Women: A Reappraisal," *Arab Studies Quarterly* 3(3):258–274.

Schlafly, Phyllis. 1981. *The Power of Positive Woman*, Cincinnati, OH: Standard Publications.

Schlegel, Alice. 1977. *Sexual Stratification*, New York: Columbia University Press.

Simmel, Georg. 1955. *Conflict: The Web of Group Affiliations*, New York: Free Press.

Simpson-Hebert, M. 1990. "Women, Food and Hospitality in Iranian Society," in Elvio Angeloni (Ed.), *Anthropology*, Guilford, CT: Dushkin Publishing Group.

Slocum, Sally. 1975. "Woman the Gatherer: Male Bias in Anthropology," in Rayna Reiter (Ed.), *Toward an Anthropology of Women*, 36–50, New York: Monthly Review Press.

Speer, James. 1984. "A Study in Political Contrasts," in David Bromley and Anson Shupe (Eds.), *New Christian Politics*, 19–41, Macon, GA: Mercer University Press.

Statistical Center of Iran. 1987. *National Census of Population and Housing, 1986*, Tehran: Statistical Center of Iran, Plan and Budget Organization.

Sullivan, E. 1986. *Women in Egyptian Public Life*, Syracuse, NY: Syracuse University Press.

Sweet, L. 1974. "In Reality: Some Middle Eastern Women," in Matthiasson (Ed.), *Many Sisters*, New York: Free Press.

Tabari, A. 1982. "Islam and the Struggle for Emancipation of Iranian Women," in A. Tabari and N. Yeganeh (Eds.), *In the Shadow of Islam: The Women's Movement in Iran*, 5–26, London: Zed Press.

Tabari, A. and Yeganeh (Eds.). 1982. *In the Shadow of Islam: The Women's Movement in Iran*, London: Zed Press.

Tapper, Richard and Nancy Tapper. 1987. "'Thank God We're Secular!' Aspects of Fundamentalism in a Turkish Town," in Lionel Caplan (Ed.), *Studies in Religious Fundamentalism*, 51–78, New York: State University of New York Press.

Time. 1985. "Jerry Falwell's Crusade," September, 2:48–57.

Tucker, J. 1985. *Women in Nineteenth-century Egypt*, Cambridge, MA: Cambridge University Press.

University of Tehran. 1985. *Admission Handbook*, Tehran.

Webber, Jonathan. 1987. "Rethinking Fundamentalism: The Readjustment of Jewish Society in the Modern World," in Lionel Caplan (Ed.), *Studies in Religious Fundamentalism*, 95–121, New York: State University of New York Press.

Weber, Max. 1946. "The Social Psychology of the World Religions," in Hans Gerth and C. Wright Mills (Trans. and Eds.), *From Max Weber: Essays in Sociology*, 284–285, New York: Oxford University Press.

Webster's New World Dictionary of the American Language. 1978. New York: World Publishing Company.

Welch, Susan. 1975. "Support Among Women for the Issues of the Women's Movement," *Sociological Quarterly* 16:216–227.

White, E. 1978. "Legal Reforms as an Indicator of Women's Status in Muslim Nations," in Beck and Keddie (Eds.), *Women in the Muslim World*, 52–69, Cambridge, MA: Harvard University Press.

Williams, J. 1979. "A Return to the Veil in Egypt," *Middle East Review* 3:49–54.

Women Living under Muslim Laws. 1991a. "ASWA Dissolution/ Update," 19-11-91, Paris, France.

Women Living under Muslim Laws. 1991b. "ASWA Update," 17-10-91, Paris, France.

World Bank. 1988. *World Tables 1987*, Washington, DC: Bank of Reconstruction and Development.

Youssef, N.H. 1974. *Women and Work in Developing Societies*, Berkeley: Institute of International Studies, University of California.

Zapot, Patricia. 1991. "Early Church Had Women Priests, Researcher Believes," *The Mirror*, November 8:16.

Zewer, Robert. 1984. "The New Christian Right and the 1980 Election," in David Bromley and Anson Shupe (Eds.), *New Christian Politics*, 173–195, Macon, GA: Mercer University Press.

Zubaida, Sami. 1987. "The Quest for the Islamic State: Islamic Fundamentalism in Egypt and Iran," in Lionel Caplan (Ed.), *Studies in Religious Fundamentalism*, 25–50, New York: State University of New York Press.

Zan-e-Rouz. "Women Researchers, High Productivity, Great Problems," 7-11-92, No. 1384 (16-8-1371):10–12.

Index